La Frontera:
Reflections on Borders in American Culture

Edited by

Judit Ágnes Kádár and András Tarnóc

La Frontera:
Reflections on Borders in
American Culture

Edited by

Judit Ágnes Kádár and András Tarnóc

© 2016 Szeged, AMERICANA eBooks

General editors: Réka M. Cristian & Zoltán Dragon

© Judit Ágnes Kádár and András Tarnóc

ISBN: 978-615-5423-35-2 (.mobi); 978-615-5423-34-5 (.epub);
978-615-5423-33-8 (PoD)

Language editors: Kenneth Stevens (Texas Christian University)
and Gabriel Melendez (University of New Mexico).

Cover by Emese Zámbó
Book design: Zoltán Dragon

AMERICANA eBooks is a division of *AMERICANA – E-Journal of American
Studies in Hungary*, published by the Department of American Studies,
University of Szeged, Hungary.
http://ebooks.americanaejournal.hu

TABLE OF CONTENTS

ABOUT THE AUTHORS

Emily Cammack is a doctoral candidate in American Studies at the University of New Mexico. Her research and teaching interests include the history of and the contemporary conditions engendered by the convergence of culture and technology in border regions. Believing that borders can be broadly defined and discriminately deployed, Emily sees the border itself as a technology that defines and destroys, confines and confounds, tricks and transcends. She is currently working to discover a vocabulary for describing, exploring, and negotiating traditional and speculative iterations of American political, economic, and cultural successes and failures in border regional contexts by considering the vernacular and intangible value systems immanent within them. Her dissertation, *Asylum, Retablos, and Bling: Border Performativity and the American Fantastic*, revisits the surreal as a specifically American response to borders in the neoliberal age.

Rafael A. Martínez is a Ph.D. student in American Studies at the University of New Mexico and also a Teaching Assistant in the American Studies and in the Chicana and Chicano Studies at the same university. He completed his MA degree at UNM in American Studies finishing his thesis, "Counter Culture Youth: Immigrant Rights Activism and the Undocumented Youth Vanguard." His analysis of the Undocumented Youth Movement sheds light on formations of civil rights activism within youth and identity formations that contest normative formations of citizenship. Rafael has a variety of interests in the areas of comparative cultural studies, critical race and class studies, critical regionalism, transnationalism, colonialism, globalism, neoliberalism and Indigeneity with particular interest in studying the collaborations of different ethnic groups in social movements and demonstrations and looks to expand his project on the Undocumented Youth Movement into a future dissertation. As an *undocuscholar*, his research and activism seeks to bring immigrant communities out of the shadows they are often relegated to.

Zoltán Peterecz earned his Ph.D. in 2010 at Eötvös Loránd University, Budapest and currently teaches courses in American history and civilization in the American Studies Department at Eszterházy Károly College, Eger. His main field of research is American history, American foreign policy, and American-Hungarian relations in the interwar years. He publishes regularly

1

in various journals on these topics. His book entitled *Jeremiah Smith, Jr. and Hungary, 1924–1926: the United States, the League of Nations, and the Financial Reconstruction of Hungary* came out in 2013.

Kitti Somogyi has been attending the University of Pécs since 2007. She finished her BA in American Literary and Cultural Studies in 2011, completed MA in English and Irish Literary and Cultural Studies two years later and started her PhD studies at the Department of Modern Literatures in 2014. The focus of her research is nineteenth century literature, especially western writings and Cormac McCarthy's works. Currently she also teaches in the Teacher Training program at the Department of English Culture and Literature, University of Pécs.

Kenneth Stevens

Kenneth Stevens is professor of history at Texas Christian University where he teaches courses on American Constitutional History and the American Presidency. In 2014, he was the Országh László Chair in American Studies at the University of Debrecen as a Fulbright Scholar. His current research project is a diplomatic history of the Republic of Texas.

András Tarnóc

András Tarnóc currently serves as Head of the Department of American Studies at Eszterházy Károly College of Eger where he teaches courses on American history, culture, literature, and government. His main research interests include settler-Indian relations in the colonial period, the dynamics of multicultural societies, and the slave narrative. He earned his Ph.D. in 2011, and was awarded habilitation by the University of Debrecen in 2013 with the habilitation thesis entitled *The Indian Captivity Narrative as the Cornerstone of the American Origination Myth* (2016) that explored the literary, historical, psychological, and educational aspects of narratives of confinement reflecting the experiences of mostly white captives of Amerindians. Recently his research has focused on the field of autobiographical literature with special emphasis on the cultural significance of antebellum slave narratives treating the latter both as examples of life writing and texts of travel. He works also as editor-in-chief of the *Eger Journal of American Studies*. His publications have appeared in journals such as *AMERICANA e-Journal of American Studies in Hungary*, *Hungarian Journal of English and American Studies*, and the *Eger Journal of American Studies*; his monograph on *The Dynamics of American Multiculturalism: a Model-Based Study* came out in 2005.

Gábor Tillman

Gábor Tillman is PhD student at the University of Pécs. His main area of research includes 19th and 20th century American culture and related literature with special interest in hero and trickster figures, and the impact of these personalities on history, society, popular culture and literature.

Kristen S. Valencia

Kristen S. Valencia is currently a PhD Candidate in the Department of American Studies at the University of New Mexico in Albuquerque, New Mexico. Her work and research on the United States-Mexico border is focused specifically on the sister cities of Nogales, Arizona and Nogales, Sonora, commonly referred to as Ambos Nogales (both Nogales). Having been born and raised in Ambos Nogales, it is crucial for Kristen to uncover histories and aid in filling gaps where historical information about the sister cities is missing. Much research about the border is centered on the populations who cross the political demarcation, as opposed to the peoples who reside at the territory line. It is Kristen's intention to focus on the lived experiences and rich historical interactions that fuel the cross-border connections and camaraderie still celebrated in Ambos Nogales today.

Tamás Vraukó

Tamás Vraukó is a senior lecturer at the Department of English, University of Miskolc; formerly worked at the College of Nyíregyháza for 23 years. He graduated from the University of Debrecen as a teacher of English and Hungarian language and literature, earned a second diploma in British Studies from the University of Warsaw and Ruskin College, Oxford, a doctoral degree in linguistics from the University of Debrecen and a PhD in Hispanic Studies from the University of Warsaw. His research areas focus on Hispanic-American history, culture and literature, and the translation process. His translations of novels, plays, and history books amount to eleven volumes so far.

PREFACE

The forthcoming essays have one common denominator, the discussion of the concept of the border in American culture. Partly motivated by a symposium held on this very topic in late 2014 at Eszterházy Károly University of Applied Sciences of Eger, Hungary, the subsequent call for papers resulted in a variety of submissions. The starting point of all essays was Gloria Anzaldua's statement: "[B]orderlands are not specific to the [American] Southwest. In fact the borderlands are physically present wherever two or more cultures edge each other, where people of different races occupy the same territory, where under, lower, middle and upper classes touch, where the space between two individuals shrinks with intimacy."

As a whole the nine articles involved treat issues related to the actual U.S.–Mexico border and U.S.-Canadian border, investigate the consequences of the encounter of different cultures, and examine the borderlines discernible in popular culture including film and music, literature, i.e. slave narratives and history.

Consequently, *Kristin Valencia* delves into the history of transboundary relations between sister cities at the Arizona-Mexico border, Nogalés, AZ and Nogales, Sonora, while *Gábor Tilman* presents an intriguing account of the life of Sam Patch the first American daredevil performing his dangerous feats at the Niagara Falls spawning over the U.S.-Canadian border. As for popular culture *Emily Cammack* explores how the classic American television show, "The Wild Wild West" is reimagined in the world of the steampunk, while *Rafael Martinez* examines film-based renderings of Mexican and Central American immigrants' efforts at entering the U.S. and *Tamás Vraukó* investigates the role of country music in Southwestern culture. *Kitti Somogyi* dissects Cormack McCarthy's dystopic frontier concept, while *András Tarnóc* examines how the encounter between the slave and the religious and cultural artifacts of the slaveholder amounts to crossing the border between oral and written culture. As far as the historical component is concerned *Kenneth Stevens* retraces ideological and political developments behind the independence struggle of Texas, while *Zoltán Peterecz* investigates the connection between American exceptionalism and the Mexican-American War.

4

Although border-related discussions in general tend to emphasize the border's capability to separate and divide, a closer look reveals that regardless of the respective cultural, economic, or political positions borderlines present a common link, a means of connection. Consequently, Ambos Nogales represent an effort to maintain cultural and personal links between two cities at opposing sides burdened by a shared history, Sam Patch was not a simple daredevil, but one of the several manifestations of the American hero living in the collective unconscious of all Americans. Furthermore, while the latest version of "The Wild, Wild West" cannot break away from a stereotype-ridden past, it focuses on one of the standard images of North American culture, the western hero. Country music, seemingly a prerogative of white southwesterners commemorates the suffering of the braceros, or Mexican agricultural workers, while the two essays focusing on events related to the breakout of the Mexican-American War dissect episodes linking the two countries' past and future.

EMILY CAMMACK

CROSSING BORDERS, STEAMPUNK, AND THE QUEER ART OF FAILURE: BARRY SONNENFELD'S *WILD WILD WEST*

This text examines visual twinnings that occur because of and within film adaptations, film remakes, and transgenre cinematic revampings. By examining "mutual immanences," "twinnings," and the frictions that occur because of and during remakes, it becomes possible to "cross borders, keep moving, and maintain a different sense of organization, sense of repetition, and embodiment of time" (Herr 12). Although I would like to find that future echoes of past works document augmentations and accretions that transcend the stultified persistence of classed, raced, and gendered stereotypes, these stereotypes persist, despite radical cinematic interventions including steam engines, fetishized gadgets, and punk aesthetics, that are supposed to combine to project science fictional speculations of alternate realities. The retro-futuristic kitsch of steampunk, in the case Barry Sonnenfeld's 1999 film *Wild Wild West*, for example, remains entrenched in post-World War Two hyper-sexualized exotica, reifying the paternalistic infantilization and erasure of ethnicity that has been endemic in the Western film genre since the turn of the twentieth century. Combining postcolonial and critical cultural critiques, this paper explores not the evolution but the devolution of border regional cinema, where the persistence of the Western's tropes, polarities, and mythologies continue to cinematically define border imaginaries.

Perhaps the "problem" for those of us who at times enjoy the escapism of a genre flick is that what we escape into is more of the same, even when dressed up in steampunk's technologized Victorian erotica or sexy strap-ons of futuristic bionic enhancements. The same story lines and the same characters persist, or resist, embodiment as anything other than a tired projection of infantilized male fantasies. I want to believe that science fiction Westerns, or Western science fictions, can and will transcend the formulae that have remained successful, or successfully overwhelming, for the past century. But the dominance of the mass produced and mass marketed audience pleasers continue to reify the generic underpinnings of the individual conquering hero who colonizes and settles frontier after frontier after frontier. Although exceptions exist, this paper compares two examples of steampunk iterations of the Western film genre to demonstrate that, while the punk aspirations and technological innovations of these films allegedly "cross borders," temporally, spatially, and even ideologically, they remain echoes of racist and masculinist frontier-era desires that manifest as the perpetual destiny of once and future film goers.

Steampunk Retrofits

Steampunk, in general, retrofits the hybridity of Victorian-inspired technofantasies with (un)common tales of science fiction and historical narrative that revision the world with an almost seamless integration of extraordinary steampowered machinery and social vision. The meanings derived from and invested in steampunk aesthetics and logics have come to be associated with innovation, unconventionality, and resistance (Miller and Taddeo xvi). Its diverse accoutrements, and its (potentially) dialectical engagement with visions of the past and versions of the future manifest in a productive dissonance that intend to interrogate the relationship between man (and woman) and machine. In film, steampunk is itself an extension or augmentation of the "social problem" film that developed as a genre during Hollywood's golden era, often echoing the reformist agenda of the late nineteenth and early twentieth centuries (Siemann 14). As such, despite their technological innovations, many of the solutions proposed within the steampunk milieu often run the staid gamut of heteronormative and progressive narratives of development, human rights, and individual integrity that were gaining ground as rallying cries at the liberal turn of the twentieth century. Steampunk cinema has also provided a venue for challenging gender normativity as well, yet certain structures remain in place. The Victorian corset, for example, under steampunk logics can be envisioned as a piece of body armor, a garment of liberation and transgression (Taddeo 53), and a fetishization of constriction and construction evocative of a costume period cyborgian erotic fantasy. Aspects of steampunk alterity suggest that anyone can find fulfillment in a world shaped by technology, where normative strictures exist to be transgressed via technological assistance (Pagliasotti 72-73). Unfortunately, not all steampunk alternate universes are created equal, and in the examples briefly reviewed below, the potential for steampunk's transgressive promise finds itself subsumed within the generic tropes it purports to circumvent.

The Wild Wild West as Steampunk Surreality

In the sixties, the television series *The Wild Wild West* demonstrated that brotherly love could and should be publicly extended via technological appurtenances. A dark, almost *noir*-ish series that challenged 'acceptable' levels of televised violence, *The Wild Wild West* set two secret service agents, with a trusty black side-kick played by Sammy Davis, Jr., against the foes of a post-bellum U.S. led by the one-and-only Ulysses S. Grant. There are all sorts of comments to be made regarding the social and historical context of this series and its four-year run during the U.S.'s short Civil Rights movement. But its proto-steampunk engagement with dandyism and gadgetry set the state for subsequent iterations of the genre, including its expressions of homoerotic fascinations with fashion, technological apparatuses that function as stand-ins for all sorts of confidence issues, and the blatant perpetuation of racial and gendered stereotypes associated with the Western genre more broadly.

Dashing and debonair Jim West (Robert Conrad), who always wore a black hat, and Artemus Gordon (Ross Martin), the white-hatted master of disguise and the civilized and brilliant brains behind the brawn, accompanied by their trusty iron horse, a steam locomotive called the Wanderer, were always ready to defend and serve the U.S. Their adventures found them pitted against nefarious technological devices first, and the evil masterminds who invented them second, emphasizing the fetish of technology that drove the series, despite the superficial claims of deep loyalty and implicit trust with which the two protagonists lip-serviced each other. West and Gordon's arch nemesis was the wily Dr. Miguelito Quixote Loveless (Michael Dunn), a diabolical dwarf, who, despite his small stature, was the most persistent and effective troublemaker encountered by West and Gordon throughout the series' duration. The show incorporated classic Western elements with spy thrillers, science fiction, alternate histories, and a certain amount of camp. In the tradition of James Bond, there were always beautiful women, clever gadgets, and delusional arch-enemies with half-insane plots to take over the country or the world.

In "The Night of the Murderous Spring," from Season 1 of the series, the ideas of crossing thresholds, doubling, and homoerotic intimacy within the show manifest when Loveless drugs West with a powerful hallucinogen. Through a mirrored window, Loveless watches West strip and shave. The viewer has the uncanny and doubled pleasure of watching West's face and torso reflected back toward Loveless as he sits in an afghan covered wheelchair in the adjacent room. Loveless gleefully tells his assistant, a giantess of a woman name Kitty, that soon West will be stripped of his humanity, his civilization, turned into a monster not in control of his own violent tendencies. Although steampunk seems to incline itself toward

Victorian gothic revivalism, steampunk's synthesis of man and machine, in an early cyborgian tendency, also taps into the *unheimlich* thrill of something that is familiar yet strange, a doubled incarnation of corporeality whose presence creates a *frisson*, a shudder, and a pause (Freud 143). In this scene, the doubling occurs not so much through a mechanical appurtenance as through the visual technology of doubled mirrors, altered vision, and the power of psychotropics. West's power resides in the simplicity of his stripped down manhood, in his exemplary rendition of Western masculine individualism and its ability to confront and conquer the wild lawlessness found at the edge of empire. The viewer waits with increasing anxiety for West's civilized facade to crumble, and when it falls, it's not clear whether we're *in* West's hallucination or merely witness to it. This episode of *The Wild Wild West* sees West defeated despite his masculine physicality and his access to technological ingenuity. The multiple mirrored repetitions create the illusion wherein West becomes lost, displaying one of the darker facets of steampunk: the doppelgänger in the shadows, the double in the mirror, and the darkness within that even the best technological enhancements can't eradicate. What this episode doesn't touch on, however, is the Freudian obsession with the automaton, the mechanical Other, a presence that titillates and terrifies in its strange yet opaque familiarity.

Sonnenfeld's *Wild Wild West* and the Queer Art of Failure

The cyborgian tendency of steampunk to enhance, alter, and transcend the material conditions of the industrial (and information) revolution, globalizing (neo)capitalism, and (post)modern imperial conquests speaks to the problematic, pernicious, and provocative potential of steampunk's generative assemblages. Whether psychotropic or steampowered, these alternative realities are, in a sense, queer potentialities that excavate the sometimes convivial relationship that exists between U.S. frontier exceptionalism and hegemonic structures that produce epistemologies and taxonomies of discrete normative and non-normative subjects. Although some subjects may feel technologically liberated some of the time, being caught in the tractor beam of U.S. exceptionalism codifies the dialectical production of difference that works to always produce a pathologically perverse Other. In other words, while steampunk cyborg alternatives queer the rules for some, they foreclose the rules for others, and, in the end, the status quo is reinvoked.

The work of Jasbir K. Puar is helpful in disassembling and unearthing the assumptions, conventions, bodies (of knowledge) that undergird the production of hetero- and homonormative U.S. subjectivities. Although Puar does not write about steampunk, and although steampunk alterities are not necessarily always or often identified as queer, her work explicitly articulates how steampunk and queer aesthetics can be mutually constitutive. In *Terrorist Assemblages*, Puar argues that queerness, as a process of assemblage, can resist facile subjectivization (206). Yet Puar also acknowledges the latent potential within queerness to retain the potential for a "dual movement" (46) that also "underscores contingency and complicity with dominant formations" (205), reinscribing conventional, uncritical productions of acceptable, rather than exceptional, subjectivities. I suggest that steampunk intends to operate similarly to queerness, in that steampunk intends to function more as an intentional process rather than a finished product. Yet the fetishized quality of steampunk's historical materialism and its predilection to eroticize classed, raced, and gendered subjects renders its subjects as perpetual victims of the power systems they initially endeavor to transcend. Puar's use of "assemblage" also evokes particular resonance with steampunk's predilection to aggregate anachronistic effects in practical, as in material, augmentation of a singular subjective experience. Assemblage, as a concept, is neither a finite noun nor an explicit verb, but rather a noun that references action. Assemblage is a process of transitional and transitory amalgamations in a spatio-temporal relationality, a geography of queered and queering differentiation that, in resisting and defying the exceptionalism of U.S. imperial, racialized, and sexualized violence, works within uneven topographies (205). Steampunk attempts something similar, although the assemblages assembled in the guise of the steampunk aesthetic often revert to normative identity structures encrusted with iron, lace, gears, cogs, and levers.

Barry Sonnenfeld's film version of *The Wild Wild West* television series, *Wild Wild West*, starring Will Smith as Jim West, Kevin Kline as Gordon, and Kenneth Branagh as Dr. Loveless, embodies the worst of steampunk assemblages in its overt and explicit refusal for the queering potential of assemblage and the defiance immanent within steampunk. Although some have attempted to redeem the film's camp and schlock by pointing to its sad attempts at racial, gendered, and ableist critiques, these fail as miserably as Donald Sterling's recent ravings against Magic Johnson in his pathetic efforts to exonerate decades of his own racial and sexist violence. The social, cultural, and even political critique initiated in the best episodes of the proto-steampunk innovations of *The Wild Wild West* television series are, in the film version, sublimated beneath a veneer of fatuous stand up gags couched in Victorian-esque fetishes and sexualized conflations of man (or woman) and machine. If this potentially cyborgian synthesis transcended or even crossed borders, genre, gender, or otherwise, then the 1999 film could be said to put into practice those elements of steampunk that might make of it a subcultural classic, but Sonnenfeld's directorial narrative instead emphasizes the intertextual limitations of the Western and steampunk cinematic genres.

For example, Artemus Gordon, the master of disguise and the brilliant inventor, whose intelligence precludes his ability to maintain successful social interactions. Of course, "successful social interactions" refers to heterosexual male prowess, which is the default purview specifically embodied by Will Smith as Jim West, a tall virile black man, often shirtless, who crossdresses at the end of the film as Ebonia, a bellydancing dominatrix given to lap dances and slap fights. Gordon, a white man, is portrayed as effeminate, emasculated by his intelligence and his curious precocity for problem solving in the realm of fantastical possibilities. We are first introduced to his character when he is in drag as a big-boned saloon girl whose "falsies" transform into pugilistic fists at the push of a button. Later, Gordon "knits" a bulletproof chain mail vest for West, takes notes instead of drawing a firearm, and cooks gourmet meals. While Gordon's inventions, adaptations, and behaviors could partake of the cultural critique that is supposedly immanent within steampunk, with its do-it-yourself mentality and its alleged propensity for social transgression, as they are portrayed in the film Gordon's creations and creativity suggest instead a sexual lack, for which or because of which he overcompensates with technological gadgets that don't always work the way they're supposed to. These failures are supposed to be funny, yet as the film progresses they are increasingly painful to watch, because Gordon's character is well-intentioned, generous, and considerate, traits that further undermine his ability to embody the full masculinity incarnated by his partner, Jim West.

West, meanwhile, is more man than even he himself can handle. Unwilling to encumber his virility with over-accessorizing, West wears a formfitting black jacket and dungarees, resists donning a disguise to work undercover, and always gets his girl…as long as she is a woman of color. When Gordon and West are assigned to the same case, the apprehension of former confederate and half-man Dr. Loveless, they descend upon New Orleans for a masked ball that serves as Loveless's 'coming out' party. Because West refuses to perform as anything other than himself, he quickly draws the attention of Miss East, played by Bai Ling, Dr. Loveless's personal assistant. Loveless, who is literally half a man, as he lost everything from the waist down fighting for the Confederacy during the U.S. Civil War, has an entire harem of apparently brilliant if underdressed female assistants. With names like Miss East (Bai Ling), Amazonia (Frederique Van Der Wal), Munitia (Musetta Vander) and Miss Lippenreider (Sofia Eng), the supposed national affinity between Loveless and the second German empire cannot be missed, especially as Loveless's megalomaniacal posturings include the adoption of a Prussian spiked helmet halfway through the film.

Gordon's apparent sexual ambivalence and West's overt masculinity are perhaps intended to challenge the Western film genre's racial and gender stereotypes, yet one of the most uncomfortable scenes in the film, a New Orleans masked ball, demonstrates that the film's steampunk veneer changes nothing in how the races and the sexes relate. At one point in the festivities, the obtuse West approaches a large redheaded woman and pounds her breasts as if they were a pair of bongos, believing that the woman is Gordon in drag. But the redhead is *not* Gordon, who has chosen to dress instead as a French trapper, an allusion both to France's loss of the Louisiana territory to U.S. imperial designs as well as to the conflation of indigenous affect with the concept of an emasculated savagery that was understood as other, or less than, red-blooded and rednecked U.S. masculinity. It is worth noting here that the only other overt reference to Native American culture and history, in a film which attempts (I think) and fails (I know) to make postmodern and ironic references the to historical period evoked in the film, is Loveless's single male companion, Hudson, a Native American, played by Rodney A. Grant. Hudson is ubiquitous, silent, wears two long braids, and is killed by West on top of a hurtling train as they speed west toward Promontory Point, UT.

When West finishes pounding on the redhead's breasts, he discovers that she is a sworn and stout Confederate belle as she screams, drops her mask, and slaps him. The crowd responds, as would be expected, in a frenzy to lynch West. West is dragged out to a hanging tree, where in an attempt to ameliorate the crowd, he again works as a sexual predator by verbally victimizing the redhead in order to deflect attention from his own racialization. Every man in the crowd nods his head in agreement with West's jabs at the woman's size and unattractiveness. Two things in this scene irreparably rupture the steampunk fantasy for which I am usually willing to suspend much disbelief and even a little cynicism. The first is the continued level of sexualized exploitation levied at women, or individuals perceived to be women. The second is that sexualized violence appears to be the great racial equalizer in this film, at least until the racialized Other crosses the race line. No amount of technological gadgetry or queer assemblage is going to salvage what could have been an homage to the original series once these lines are crossed. And they are crossed, over and over and over again. Will Smith's portrayal of a black Jim West at the mercy of a lynching crowd evokes the same depths of uncanny horror as the postcard unearthed and re-rendered by Ken González-Day. Here, I reference the stunning, striking work of González-Day, who, similar to Afrosurrealist visual artist Kara Walker, refuses to dissemble the histories of racialized and sexualized violence that has been and still is commodified into codified silence and complicity evident in the post card of a hanging sold as a souvenir. What is more horrific, the photographic evidence of racialized violence, or its erasure? The dynamic, if not dialectic, tension between these two options evokes the exceptional horror intimated at in *The Wild Wild West* television episode discussed above: the doubling and mirrored yet opaque surface of the hallucination, something familiar yet strange, a dislocation relative to something once though familiar but now totally alien. And yet again, I point to the gloss of steampunk's alleged alterity as the means, the method, and the justification for the egregious conflation of sexualized violence with racialized violence.

Another steampunk assemblage of technology and sexuality is Sonnenfeld's revisioning of the original Loveless as a double amputee with the suggestion that, without his nether parts, Loveless is unsexed but never emasculated in the terms of Gordon's overt feminization. Several shots as well as verbal references throughout the film make clear to the viewer Loveless's "use of mechanology" to invent "hard pumping, indefatigable steeliness," in reference to the various devices he uses to conquer the world and also the bedroom. Whereas Artemus Gordon's steampunk accessories tend to be intellectual rather than visceral props, Loveless takes the hypermasculinity of West's persona and extrudes it into an exoskeleton of moving, grinding, steaming parts. This is best evinced when he retreats to a remote canyon in Monument Valley, Arizona, the iconic setting for many Western films, to create a steam-powered spider. If he had traveled a little further south to Chinle, Arizona, Loveless could have located his giant steampunk spider near the lair of the Navajo Spider Woman at Spider Rock, a towering sandstone obelisk in Canyon de Chelly and home to one of the most revered and powerful mythological forces in Navajo cosmology. The film's most obvious and perverted reference to steampunk sensibility, Loveless's eight-legged contraption emerges from its red stone abyss to stamp its way across the western landscape, carrying Loveless and his assistants toward a rendezvous with President Grant at Promontory Point, UT, the fabled site of the joining of the Union and Central Pacific railheads in the completion of the first U.S. transcontinental railroad. If anything in the film demonstrates Sonnenfeld's limited understanding of the potential radicalism of steampunk's industrial technological intervention, this towering spider is it.

Sonnenfeld treats disability (similar to race, gender, and sexuality) as if it is something to be mocked in order to raise a cheap laugh. In the film, disability is imagined as something undesirable, something that can and should be cured or overcome, and something without a future and therefore outside time. Alison Kafer argues that the seeming inevitability of these assumptions have been naturalized, thereby depoliticizing and effectively erasing disability from public awareness, responsibility, and debate, similar to the erasure González-Day evokes in the re-rendered photographs above. Similar to Jasbir Puar's arguments regarding queer assemblages, Kafer argues that disability itself is an assemblage, a collection of affinities, and a site of and for questions that point to a futurity of and for disability rather than a finite ending, status, condition, or definition. Kafer also challenges feminist, queer, and crip assumptions about disability in terms that reference Donna Haraway's cyborg theory as one that essentializes disability experience by assuming that technology fixes everything and fits everyone. Yet Kafer suggests that the cyborg is redeemable, as long as it is "cripped," or as long as its faults, gaps, and oversights are acknowledged. Cyborgs, too, are assemblages, unpredictable and fluid, mimicking the condition and movement of the crip. In other words, the cyborg can be adapted to articulate and explore crip potentialities, where the crip does not always have to become an appurtenance to the cyborg (116).

The articulations between Puar's queer and Kafer's crip provides a critique that problematizes the cyborgian aggregates within which Loveless has inserted himself. Conforming to the hegemonic and maniacal demands of a frontier culture, whose mythologies aim ever toward a teleology of white heteronormative abilities, Loveless forces what is left of his body into a cyborgian contortion that projects his masculine virility through the escalating fire power of his steam-driven intentions and inventions. Yet his final gambit at overcompensation "fails," as his cyborg spider cripples itself due to its "unpredictability," its fluidity, and its propensity to "mimic" the condition and movement of the crip. This failure of Loveless's mechanical augmentation provides one of the most interesting and surreal moments of the film. As Loveless escapes from Promontory Point with President Grant, who has refused to sign over the territorial U.S., West and Gordon attempt a rescue that sends West into the belly of the arachnid beast for a "whupping." While in its bowels, a constricted and cacophonous place of gears, levers, and chains, West encounters a seemingly endless horde of white men whose industrial accidents, or Loveless's tampering, have left less than human. In a strange echo of the television series, when Loveless had barely been able to wait for West to succumb to the dehumanizing and decivilizing effects of a hallucinogenic shaving cream, in the film version West is confronted by an exteriorization of uncanny and dehumanized automatons, beings who are half men and half machine, and whose intellects, if they had any to begin with, are essentially negated under the extreme immiseration of the life of a worker whose value is extracted in form of alienable labor. The men are themselves alien and altered, with blades for hands, metal plates for heads, and mad kung fu fighting skills, learned from Chinese coolies. The ultimate embodiment of the effects of manual labor under the industrialized system, these men shoveling coal into the spider's boilers have been integrated into the machinery of the interior workings of Loveless's killing machine. In an inverse of the other characters in the film, who augment themselves with various exterior articulations of steampunk embellishment, the men West fights in the sublevels of the machine's innards are appurtenances of *its* technology, the organic ruptures that queer its mechanical drive toward Loveless's vision of future division.

In *The Queer Art of Failure*, Judith Halberstam, interested in Freud's discussion of the uncanny as the return of the repressed, similar to the strains of subversion hinted at in *The Wild Wild West* television episode discussed above, explores the queering of "common sensical" ideological systems, the aesthetics of reproduction and repetition, and low culture. Looking at popular cultural productions, Halberstam identifies failure as a place, space, process, and practice of collective nonconformity, which also functions as a queer aesthetic. At the risk of suggesting that the film *Wild Wild West* is a queer success narrative because of its failures, I suggest it is also possible to think about the queer advantage of failure in terms of steampunk, which works to recast normative success stories as cyclical redundancies. In both cases, failure marks the potential for creative liberation. Halberstam asserts that something is possible in failure, even if it is loss, illegibility, confusion, desperation, or death. I want to embrace Halberstam's optimism, yet I find the despair and antagonism of pessimism to be more appropriate when encountering the uncanny surrogates of violences past, especially as they are reiterated in Barry Sonnenfeld's *Wild Wild West*. Where *Wild Wild West* fails is in its endeavors to evoke the success of the steampunk genre, and where it succeeds is in the reification of the tired, yet still ideologically violent, tropes of genre films. Which ultimately means, it fails.

WORKS CITED

Freud, Sigmund. (2003) *The Uncanny*. Trans. David McClintock. New York: Penguin Books.

González-Day, Ken. "Franklin Avenue." Photograph. *New York Times*, 6 Dec. 2012. Web. 27 Oct. 2015.

---. "The Original Version of Franklin Avenue." Photograph. *New York Times*, 6 Dec. 2012. Web. 27 Oct. 2015.

Halberstam, Judith. (2011) *The Queer Art of Failure*. Durham: Duke UP.

Haraway, Donna. (1991) *Simians, Cyborgs, and Women: The Reinvention of Nature*. New York: Routledge.

Herr, Cheryl Temple. (1996) *Critical Regionalism and Cultural Studies: From Ireland to the American Midwest*. Gainesville: UP of Florida.

Kafer, Alison. (2013) *Feminist, Queer, Crip*. Bloomington: Indiana UP.

Miller, Cynthia J. and Julie Anne Taddeo. (2013) "Introduction." *Steaming into a Victorian Future: A Steampunk Anthology*. Eds. Julie Anne Taddeo and Cynthia J. Miller. Lanham: Rowman & Littlefield. xv–xxvi.

Pagliossotti, Dru. (2013) "Love and the Machine: Technology and Human Relationships in Steampunk Romance and Erotica." Eds. Julie Anne Taddeo and Cynthia J. Miller. *Steaming into a Victorian Future: A Steampunk Anthology*. Lanham: Rowman & Littlefield. 65–85.

Puar, Jasbir K. (2007) *Terrorist Assemblages: Homonationalism in Queer Times*. Durham: Duke UP.

Siemann, Catherine. (2013) "Some Notes in the Steampunk Social Problem Novel." Eds. Julie Anne Taddeo and Cynthia J. Miller. *Steaming into a Victorian Future: A Steampunk Anthology*. Lanham: Rowman & Littlefield. 3–19.

"The Night of the Murderous Spring." *The Wild Wild West*. 15 Apr. 1966. Television.

White, Richard. (1991) *The Middle Ground: Indians, Empires, and Republics in the Great Lakes Region, 1650-1815*. Cambridge: Cambridge UP.

Wild Wild West. Directed by Barry Sonnenfeld, 1995. DVD.

RAFAEL A. MARTÍNEZ

TRANSFORMATIVE BORDERS IN CINEMA: EVOLVING CONCEPTS OF MIGRANT CROSSINGS

In the past ten years, visual artists have turned their cameras to the subjects of Latino immigration and migrants and their borders and border crossings as phenomena resulting from neoliberal economic development in the Americas. Films highlighted and discussed in this paper such as *Voces Inocentes* and *Sin Nombre* center the struggles of immigrants in overcoming geospatial and symbolic borders, poverty, and violence. These films have challenged and problematized stereotypical notions of who immigrants are, how borders are constituted, and the use of borders as metaphors for social control. Both of these films implicate US imperialism as an instigating force of violence and the U.S. as a refuge for those who are unsettled.

Filmmakers and cinema offer critical visual depictions and deconstructions of the border in physical and imagined representations. The films *Voces Inocentes* and *Sin Nombre* represent borders as more than points of intersection or crossing but as border chronotopes. In this paper, I define a border chronotope as a social domain that is constituted through social relations, economic processes and cultural formations. An analysis of the two films, *Voces Inocentes* and *Sin Nombre* provide insight into the social, political, and economic forces impelling immigration and migrants, while at the same time offering polemic constructions of family life, gender issues, modern technologies and illicit activities. The "border chronotope" at play in the two films *Voces Inocentes* and *Sin Nombre* works cinematically to redefine temporal, spatial and relational dimensions across transnational spaces. I draw on and modify the concept of "chronotope" by Russian philosopher, Mikhail Bakhtin. Bakhtin used the concept of chronotope as change over time and space (1981). I use "border chronotope" to analyze the fluidity of time and space in the US-Mexico borderlands region. These films reveal the transnational process that expands the identities of migrants, concepts of multiple borders, and underlines the socioeconomic issues that have developed a transborder network of migrants.

The idea of fixed borders is a concept historically contested by Mexican-American scholars who imagine borderlands as possessing fluid characteristics like the notion of *Greater Mexico* (Paredes 1976). More recently, the aim of borderlands studies scholars and immigration scholars has been to decenter static constrictive physical borders, and instead demonstrate how everyday cultural practices destabilize fixed structures. Immigration studies remind us that migrations have long historical patterns across generations, populations, and time frames (Lee 1998, Ngai 2004, Camacho 2008, and Pegler-Gordon 2009.

Borders and Border Crossers

The United States' borderlands as a geographic location, constantly evolves over time as people cross and re-cross political boundaries and consequently constitute and reconstitute ideas about immigration and immigrants. From the 1950s onward, the typical laborers arriving in the US were young males from Mexico and Central America. U.S. intervention in countries like El Salvador and Guatemala left Central America war stricken and dispossession of land created push factors for Latin American migration to the U.S. Similarly, economic policies like NAFTA (1994) proved to be yet another way in which U.S. intervention results in economic displacement, internal migration and out migration whether in Mexico or Central America. Many rural farmers in Mexico's interior left towns and villages, their exodus created practically ghost towns. Those left behind were left to suffer the economic depressions instigated by the neoliberal policies of NAFTA. The patterns today encompass more countries and individuals than simply Mexico. Many women and children came to depend on male migrants living in the U.S. However, over time, the economic pattern of the enterprising young male immigrant gave way to other patterns of migrations involving whole families, single women and eventually child migration for reunification. Many such efforts are for family reunification purposes. Latino immigration is a process in flux and in interplay with U.S. domestic and foreign policy and the U.S.-Mexico border is as much a reality for Central Americans as it has been for Mexico.

Over the past ten years, intense surveillance of the U.S./Mexico border resulted from domestic fears of economic and demographic impacts from immigrant numbers and alleged concerns about terrorism and the effects of the drug war. Nine Eleven became the historical landmark to impact this generation of immigrants, policy making, and scholarship production. After Nine Eleven, President George Bush, Jr. pushed Congress to pass the U.S.A. Patriotic Act (2001) that essentially provided funds to militarize and provide for large amounts of border defense construction(s). Increased surveillance has led to dangerous conditions for both; migrants crossing into the U.S. and for migrants at the border seen as impacting living conditions along the U.S./Mexico borderlands. Commercial and independent filmmakers have taken up the U.S.-Mexico border and border crossings as the subject of their films. Since the implementation of punitive immigrant and defense policies, there has been an increase of immigrants, immigrant deaths, and violence committed against immigrants coming to the U.S. The profile of the immigrant has also changed dramatically in the last ten years.

Utilizing the concept of border chronotope can add new perspectives to our understanding of immigrants and border crossings that can work to dispel negative stereotypes and propaganda regarding immigrants and immigration. Borders unite and divide populations because they serve to connect people and goods that move across nation states but are also used to contain people for purpose of social control. Thus, border chronotopes are complex social domains that entail ideological and economic processes, political ramification, and human and environmental relations. Border chronotopes offer possibilities for moving beyond geospatial formations and state control. Films such as *Voces Inocentes* and *Sin Nombre* offer visual cultural expressions that underscore how US neoliberal policies create the social and economic conditions that migrants flee- poverty, violence, oppression and exploitation- and yet become the sites of refuge that immigrants claim as a strategy for social betterment.

Push Factors: Constructing the Magnet System in *Voces Inocentes*

The film *Voces Inocentes* (2004), directed by Luis Mandoki displays push factor elements for war stricken Salvadorians dealing with the results of U.S. interventionism. The film depicts immigrant origin points for Central Americans who must choose between fighting for the revolutionary militia or the national army backed by the U.S. military. *Voces Inocentes* translates to "innocent voices" hinting at the predicament young males from the age of twelve face when they become eligible for recruitment to the Salvadoran army. The title also highlights the loss of innocence at an early age to make way for a forced early maturity process in a violent society going through its civil war. Furthermore, I read *Voces Inocentes* as a film that documents Central American youth as a new migrating demographic with historical roots tracing back to the 1980s.

Luis Mandoki is a Mexican filmmaker who started his career venturing in independent filmmaking working with a variety of Mexican non-profit organizations focusing on issues of social justice. After success in the independent area of filmmaking with films in Spanish like *El Secreto* (1980) and *Motel* (1984), Mandoki dove into full-length Hollywood productions such as *Gaby: A True Story* (1987), *When a Man Loves a Woman* (1994), and *Message in A Bottle* (1999). Mandoki would have a twenty-year gap of Spanish films from 1984 to 2004 when *Voces Inocentes* was released. As he relates in an interview the first personal challenge he had to overcome was being one of the first filmmakers working outside of Mexico while being able to produce popular films in the U.S. (Crusellas 2007). He also points to his natural push towards producing films that focused on questions related to the human condition, which is what attracted him to working with the writer of *Voces Inocentes*, Oscar Torres.

Mandoki categorizes *Voces Inocentes* as "Cine Reivindicativo" or "revindictive film," a particular style produced in Mexico during the 70s and 80s that centered on social justice issues through ideological production. *Voces Inocentes* conveys a humanist message comparing the struggle between innocence and civil war (CorreCamara 2014). The dilemma of innocence is not only posited against the issue of violence and war in the film, but also as the motive for migrating to the U.S. *Voces Inocentes* is one of the first films to expand the notion of *Greater Mexico* for immigrants of a Central American point of origin. Mandoki had the good fortune of encountering a scriptwriter suitable for the film he had in mind.

Oscar Torres drew on his own experience growing up in El Salvador during the Civil War to write the script for *Voces Inocentes*. At a lecture given at the University of California at Santa Barbara in 2011, Torres described the insatiable drive that led him to write *Voces Inocentes*. Recalling as he lay in his comfortable one bedroom apartment in Los Angeles, CA, he states, "I would wake up in the middle of the night sweating, terrified in a panic, unable to explain what was causing this anguish inside of me." He remembered feeling lost at this particular time. As he expresses he was making "films without aim." His way of life had become "Hollywoodish" and meaningless; that is, until the suppressed memories of his childhood began to emerge during his sleep. At this point, he explains he was in a professional rut, and an eviction notice served to remind him that he had hit rock bottom. Adding a bit of humor to his lecture he revealed, "Instead of paying my rent, I bought myself a computer." The computer served as a form of therapy for his soul and eventually developed into the production of *Voces Inocentes*. "I was a screenwriter. And so I wrote my emotions in the only way I knew how to do so" (Torres).

Oscar Torres' autobiographical work, *Voces Inocentes*, reflects the anguish and violent displacement Salvadorians and Central American peoples experienced beginning in the 1970s and continuing to the early 1990s. As a result of economic, social and political instability, migration from Central America increased dramatically. An increase occurred again beginning in 2013 (Krogstad and Gonzalez-Barrera 2014). The neo-conservative agenda of the 1980s embodied by former President Ronald W. Reagan, nurtured puppet governments throughout Central and South America that backed US neo-conservative policies. Reagan's economic policies pushed export-driven economics and deindustrialization. El Salvador's revolutionary party, Farabundo Martí National Liberation Front (FMLN), became dissatisfied with the governments' exploitation of its people and began to try to undo foreign influence in the country. *Voces Inocentes* captures the experience of families, women, and children that were innocent bystanders during the geopolitical conflicts of the time period. The film narrates the story of the main character, Chava, whose innocence is disrupted by the harsh realities he must face at the expense of the outbreak of the Civil War. The introductory scene reveals the setting and conditions that Chava, and many Salvadorian families found themselves in - caught between crossfires.

The film begins with a dark image and the sound of heavy rainfall; a few young boys walk in formation with their hands raised at their heads as army soldiers are leading them away. Chava's narration reveals the miserable and uncertain fate that awaits them. The scene then dissolves into a memory of Chava at the doorsteps of his home as he catches his father leaving the family for "El Norte," and never to be seen again. In the same sequence Chava announces, "She told me I had to be the man of the house… But first, I had to pee." This moment in the film illustrates to the audience that Chava is caught in the middle of a stark reality. Chava's childhood innocence is sacrificed as he assumes new responsibilities following his father's departure.

The father's departure is not explained directly in the film. However, because of the film's context, the audience is lead to assume that the father fled for his life as a result of the Civil War. Early on in the film the issue is introduced in a breakthrough scene where Chava is sitting inside the classroom admiring the beauty of one of his classmates, Rosita who he has a crush on. Unexpectedly a bomb goes off outside the classroom and sends everyone into a panic. The teacher orders everyone to take cover under the floor, but then we see the national military soldier come into the school and order everyone to get in lines outside with the rest of the students. We see children who are being placed in the back of trucks and hauled away. This scene depicts how every available male older than twelve years old during the Civil War was drafted to the national army (CorreCamara 2014). In later scenes, the audience sees that Chava has escaped the national army draft, and his uncle is trying to convince him to join the revolutionary forces. These two scenes combined demonstrate the conflict Salvadorian youth were placed in when forced to choose between two sides.

The remainder of the film depicts Chava's journey to escape persecution as the conflict intensifies and thousands of people are forced to migrate and leave their lives behind. The culminating scene shows Chava saying goodbye to his family as he is placed in the back of a pickup truck. As he leaves for El Norte, his mom tells him to promise that he will be strong. When Chava moves further from his family on the pickup truck, his younger brother innocently shouts, "I am now the man of the house!" in a joyful tone. This scene reveals the cycle of forced adulthoods and migrations across generations in violence stricken countries like El Salvador.

Rosa Linda Fregoso describes this type of forced migration narrative construction as, "a nonlinear pattern, ricocheting back and forth between different narrative spaces and times" (Fregoso 2003, 72). Chava's father was forced to leave, and we see that Chava is the second displaced generation in the family, who will be followed by his younger brother. Chava declares, "I don't want to go to the United States. But if I stay, they're going to kill me," which reveals the push factor that many Central Americans experienced during this time period. Many young men had no other option but to flee north for survival. U.S. imperialism and neo-conservative economics had direct consequences all over the hemisphere, which include economic displacement, internal migration and eventually forced migration from Latin American countries to the U.S. Consequently, the U.S. becomes a large magnet for refugees and migrants seeking shelter in the land of the free.

The "border chronotope" illustrated by *Voces Inocentes* expands previously held concepts of border crossings and immigrants. The typical migrant depicted in traditional film was the poor male Mexican crossing the U.S.-Mexico border. However, *Voces Inocentes* forces the audience to break away from such notions of fixed borders or border crossings limited to the U.S.-Mexico border, and rather allows us to consider the transnational structures in place across trans-American routes (Saldívar 2011). The chronotope in the film stretches the idea of a U.S.-Mexican border to inform the audience of hemispheric displacement or the notion of a *Greater Mexico*, and the crossing of multiple borders for safety. Over time, borders have come to be imaginary or important only for political purposes. The pressing realities of women, men, and children like Chava are downplayed in the dominant political discourse, which focuses on legal violation (Schmidt-Camacho 2011). The direct consequences and impacts of geopolitical formations become a reality and the U.S. a magnet by design.

Dark Journeys – *Sin Nombre*'s Middle Passage

Sin Nombre (2009) is a story directed by Cary Joji Fukunaga that highlights the dangerous migration conditions experienced by Central Americans and Mexicans as they plod along Mexico's railroad system on their journeys to the U.S. In several ways *Sin Nombre*, a contemporary story, is in conversation with *Voces Inocentes* because it picks up the historical trajectory of Central American migrants' push factors where Mandoki's film left off. In other words, *Sin Nombre* is a film that presents the stories of Central American subjects who face social ills that the region has been exposed to since U.S. interventionism in the 1980s.

When the wave of the first Central American immigrants reached the U.S. in the 1980s, many of them were young males arriving in urban cities like Los Angeles, Dallas, and Washington D.C. Faced with assimilation issues into U.S. culture and lack of family presence, many of them turned to the streets to find a sense of belonging in street gangs like the Mara Salvatrucha gang (MS13) (Diaz 2009). The terrifying presence of the Mara Salvatrucha sheds light on to the overarching socioeconomic creations that have plagued the hemisphere with organized crime. *Sin Nombre* shows how the gang has developed into a transnational network from its beginnings in Los Angeles, CA. After the gang began to grow in numbers and in influence, the U.S. government began to deport many of its high-ranking members back to Central American countries. The U.S. created a "double displacement;" first by economic push factors, and second by deportation and regulatory practices. After the U.S. washed its hands of these gang members through removal practices, not only did it displace people, but it also generated social issues in home countries. The U.S. created the setting for a Frankenstein-like structure to develop in its own soil and then transferred the madness of its creation to a region already plagued with overwhelming problems. Gang violence and organized crime adds a new dimension to the concepts of migration routes and brings new dangers to immigrant populations who keep getting younger and younger. Furthermore, organized crime also transforms our notion of borders and a *Greater Mexico* that is representative of intricate migration routes.

Cary Fukunaga directed and wrote the screenplay for *Sin Nombre* as the first full-length film in his career. Prior to *Sin Nombre*, Fukunaga was successful at writing and directing short films that won recognitions. In an interview Cary Fukunaga states that "this movie ten years from now, should feel like a window into this time period," (MovieCollege 2010) highlighting *Sin Nombre's* efforts to capture this moment in immigration history. And he goes on to state, "the universal aspect of people coming from a place of struggle to improve their lives," as a way that the film aims to bring dignity to the immigrant subject. Cary Fukunaga was backed by a big production company like Focus Film, which explains its wide release, but along with his partnership came creative liberty that Fukunaga used to include actual immigrant populations as extras in many of the shots of the film with efforts to present actual real lived practices and interactions.

Fukunaga describes the film in the genre of realism due to its pressing need to convey the message of the dangerous paths immigrants face. In another interview in reference to the beginning stages of his screen writing for the film he declares, "The more I did the research, the more I had the need to finish it and the responsibility to do it well" (Boriboj 2009) In that same interview Fukunaga reveals that his consciousness in the immigration subject came when he read an article about immigrants being trapped in a trailer in Texas who died from heat exposure (Fountain 2002). Fukunaga's efforts to direct his first full length film demonstrates a need to bring awareness to new immigrant issues in crossing multiple borders as a way to make it into a universal topic that larger audiences can relate to.

La Travesía de Enrique published in 2006 offers a poignant account of a young migrant driven to cross borderlines. The author, Sonia Nazario is a reporter who brings to life the story of one Honduran migrant teen (Enrique) whose experience parallels many others. Fukunaga was influenced by Nazario's work as it provided him with insight into the dangerous networks that exist in migration from Central America to the U.S. Once Nazario began her research, she realized that child migrants swarmed to the north by the thousands each day in a way that expands our current understanding of border chronotope. She was appalled that these stories were not known in the U.S. and that no human rights alerts were being raised by these forces. So in 2000, she set out to capture these tragic stories of migration first hand. She met Enrique in Nuevo Laredo, Mexico with the objective of capturing his story and witnessing the dangerous conditions experienced by migrants. Her work reveals the structures of displacement that separates millions of families across borderlines and is helpful in analysis with the *Sin Nombre*'s film.

The film's introduction of the main characters: Casper, Lil Mago and Sayra follows a transnational imagery that depicts the social issues as push factors from the Central American origin points. Casper lives in Tapachula, Chiapas, Mexico. The introductory scene begins with Casper focused on a wall-size poster of a lush, beautiful forest. The beautiful scenery is contrasted by the harsh urban barrio of Tapachula where Casper lives. In the scene, he is preparing to leave his home. His face is stern yet emotion driven with expressions that reveal bottled anguish. After Casper's introduction, the camera cuts to a direct intimidating close-up low-angle shot of Lil Mago's tattoo covered face. The camera's proximity to the subject and the tattoos are meant to present the menacing presence of the Mara Salvatrucha in the region (Diaz 2009). Lil Mago's introduction as the leader of the gang also serves to signify the violent and menacing lifestyle of the Mara Salvatrucha. The next scene introduces Sayra and her family. The scene begins with the image of Sayra looking out into her massive *favela*-style neighborhood in the Honduran capital, Tegucigalpa. The shear mass of the urban landscape places the minuscule figure of Sayra in proportion to her surroundings. However, the next scene is a shot of "La Bombilla" in

Tapachula that demonstrates the massive immigrant hub that surrounds the train station of southern Mexico. The transnational imagery used in the beginning of the film operates as another example of a border chronotope in contemporary cinema. The blurring of borders, time, and space in this film also reminds the audience that borders and migrants are not fixed constructions, but rather part of an, "illegitimate and artificial geopolitical border" (Fregoso 1993, 66).

The transition from *Voces Inocentes* to the opening scene of *Sin Nombre* is a historically continuous process that developed over time and space. Historically and contextually, *Sin Nombre* picks up in the early nineties where *Voces Inocentes* left off. In *Sin Nombre*, the structures of migration have changed to fixed intricate systems and routes with new added dangers that are part of a migrant's journey. *Greater Mexico* then, entails Mexico's vast geographical expanse that connects Central American and Mexican migrants crossing to El Norte. The idea of a *Greater Mexico* presented by *Sin Nombre* further consolidates Rosa Linda Fregoso's point, "the category of border directs our attention to the spaces 'within and between' what were once sanctified as 'homogeneous' communities" (Fregoso 1993, 65). The majority of the passage is covered by the migrants in what is known as "La Bestia" or "The Beast" – the train that connects southern Mexico all the way to border towns in northern Mexico (the country freighting system) (Nazario 2006) Riding La Bestia itself is one of the dangers of the journey, as thousands of migrants' lose limbs, body parts and many more lose their lives to the danger of train hopping going north. The Mara Salvatrucha represents one of the symbolic and realistic shadow antagonists in the film. Migrants may experience a constant state of fear and intimidation from gang members during their journey. Women and children face the possibility of sexual violence and rape. The Mara Salvatrucha serve as hit man or "middle man" in the larger picture of the drug cartels and the drug war. The title of the film *Sin Nombre* translates to "Without Name," which speaks to the unspeakable or nameless amounts of dangers that are part of contemporary migration routes.

The representation of the character Sayra and her family depicts the complex relationships created by migrant displacements. In the scene where Sayra is introduced in Tegucigalpa, she is reunited with her father who had left her when she was only a child. When he first meets Sayra after so many years away from his country, her father says, "She's already a lady." We learn that her father has come for her to take her back with him to the U.S. The landscape shot where Sayra is introduced, informs the audience of the extreme poverty that influenced her father to migrate to the U.S. That same factor served as a motive for him to return for his daughter and rescue her from poverty. Her father hopes that their journey to the U.S. will provide them with a better life. Like in the case of many other Central American migrants, economic factors are key in the migrations of Sayra's family, who migrate to the north with the hopes of being able to build a better future.

The landscape image of Tegucigalpa is nearly identical in imagery to that shown in *Voces Inocentes*; but nevertheless it serves to inform that conditions in Central America have not improved or in fact have grown worse from the period where *Voces Inocentes* leaves up to present day. Sonia Nazario paints a vivid picture when she presents the harsh story of her maid's poverty in her native Guatemala, "Ella los arrullaba con consejos para calmar las punzadas del hambre. 'Dormí boca abajo para que no te haga tanto ruido la tripa [I slept mouth down so that your gut does not make too much noise]'" (Nazario 2006, viii). Today, economic conditions continue to serve as push factors drawing immigrants to the prosperity of the center of the magnet. However, new border chronotopes are explored in *Sin Nombre* as new inherited dangers added over time and space play out in North America's *Greater Mexico*.

Throughout Sayra's journey danger waits at every corner. While aboard "La Bestia" one of the first nights of the journey, she is almost raped by Lil Mago but is saved by Casper who ends up killing Lil Mago. The death of Lil Mago represents the point of departure in the film where the audience learns about the dangers involved in crossing borders. For the rest of the film, Casper will have to face the consequences of his lifestyle as he is hounded by the Mara Salvatrucha throughout the country for killing the leader of his local chapter.

In her investigation, Sonia Nazario finds that migrant deaths are a common occurrence on the trains: "[C]on frecuencia los pandilleros arrojan del tren en movimiento a los migrantes que los hacen entrar en colera porque no tienen dinero o porque se resisten; o los dejan muertos en el techo del tren para que los encuentren los empleados ferroviarios en la proxima estacion [With frequency gang members throw migrants who upset them for not having money or for resisting from the moving train; or they leave them dead on top of the train so that the employees of the train can find them in the next station]" (Nazario 2006, 92).

Mid-point in the film, there is yet another landscape shot of a beautiful sunrise over a mountain range as the migrants are nearing the middle of their journey. The shot is contrasted again by the grim realities of migration. These scenes contrasting the past and present raise the question of why a country so rich in natural resources is in fact a trap for poverty and alienation. The scene shifts to an immigrant hub, known as "Casas del Migrante." Casas are safe houses, where hundreds of immigrants at a time are given shelter, food, a shower, aid, and supplies to assist them along their journey. The scene visually introduces the audience to the magnitude of the populations involved in these migrant streams. Casas' represents migrant resources that exist in spite of political ideas and regulations. The border chronotope is also at play with Casa del Migrante as we see that the border is not in a fixed position or location, but rather creates structures and spaces across the landscape of the hemisphere that connect migrants from one country to the other.

Transnational violence forms an important subtext of the film. The film ends with Casper being shot and killed by Smiley, a young boy whom he inducted into the Mara Salvatrucha at the beginning of the film. Before squeezing the trigger, Smiley says "La Mara for life, homie" and proceeds to execute Casper with two shots directly to the chest. Casper's death by Smiley reinforces unavoidable violence under these conditions. The common use of landscape scenery by Fukunaga in the film provides the audience with an idea of the immense structures set up in the process of migration. The transnational nature of migration forces us to consider border chronotopes that over time continue to add dimensions of violence, economies, politics, and cultures. The film ends showing Sayra now in the U.S. with a backpack and looking out in to the horizon, as a way to signify that she must now get rid of her old identity, and must look ahead at the new possibilities in the U.S. She must now find her own ways in El Norte just as Chava in *Voces Inocentes* did. However, the difference in using a female character with Sayra is remarkable because it highlights a gender shift occurring in the migrant demographics. Whereas in the early eighties and nineties the migrant was mostly represented by a young male character, the new wave of immigrants includes young women in notable numbers as well.

Sin Nombre is another example of a film that leaves the audience with the reality of violence encountered by migrants going north, but one of its unique qualities is that it is able to demonstrate the direct transnational impact that violent structures have on hemispheric communities. Charles Ramírez Berg pointing out that both sides of the film industry must be held accountable suggests that close readings are needed to investigate more fully the Anglo-centered films and the Chicano-centered ones" (Berg 1992, 48). As a critical audience, there must be interaction with the sociopolitical historical discourses that highlight the problematic meaning of transnational routes that negatively impact hemispheric and global communities.

Reflection on Border and Migrant Transformations

Films like *Voces Inocentes* and *Sin Nombre* expanded border chronotopes over time and geographic space since earlier films like *Alambrista*'s (1977). When *Alambrista* was released in the 1970s, it was a film that presented the original notion of the male Mexican migrant pursuing economic independence and prosperity. In 1990, critical cinematic reviews by David R. Maciel praised films like *Alambrista* and asked border films to "offer an alternative cinematic language, style and ideology" (Maciel 71). Similarly today, critical audiences demand that moviemakers continue to use this formula with the incorporation of new border dimensions that remain relevant to present day issues.

Voces Inocentes demonstrates that the depiction of the traditional Mexican male migrant is an outdated notion that must be revisited to include the larger processes at work that include the displacement of women, children and other Central/Latin Americans. Chava's story visually and artistically showcases the violence that affected the Central American region pushing many children, families, men and women alike to the north escaping persecution. Migration patterns from Central America have existed in large numbers from the 1970s to the present day. *Alambrista*'s focused on a particular trope of individual migration stories rather than a larger border chronotope focus. The films presented in this paper are transnational by construction, with aims at presenting the realities about geopolitical journeys that are entailed in "border crossings."

Sin Nombre is a film that shows the new dangerous dimensions that did not exist during *Alambrista's* release. One of the successes of *Alambrista* is the ability to capture the inherent dangers of the migrant's journey north and introducing an audience to the topic of immigration. David R. Maciel concludes "Roberto receives quite an education during the course of the film" (Maciel 71), to show that the dangers along the journey are part of the migrant's crude educational process. Similarly, the end of *Sin Nombre* shows Sayra reflecting on the heartbroken journey endured after going from southern to northern Mexico. Both films end showing their main characters in a state of reflection, leaving the audience to draw their own conclusions about whether economic prosperity is worth the migrant lifestyle. *Sin Nombre*'s title suggests that there is simply no vocabulary or words for the unspeakable or unnamable violent crimes, and rather remain - *sin nombre* [without name].

Perhaps the idea of a film that encompasses a full length border chronotope is realistically impossible in cinematic dimension, but it is only by maintaining the dialogue between cinematic representations of borders in communication with literature that we can represent new and dynamic dimensions of borders more fully. Films like *Voces Inocentes* and *Sin Nombre* continue to engage audiences with new critical ideas of borders and migrants. We continue to see that a transnational and trans-American scope is needed to understand the historical processes that develop along migration patterns at the U.S.-Mexico borderland and beyond. Rosa Linda Fregoso declares, "The normalcy of state terrorism in our own historical moment makes the movement for global social justice more urgent than ever before" (Fregoso 2003, xv). Fregoso underscores an imperative in new border studies. The stakes are high, and the number of people affected continues to rise; thus, the evolution of border and migrant identities continues in a cycle. The world continues to be more interconnected than ever before, and cinema can be a useful tool to bring humanity closer to a more harmonious future.

WORKS CITED

Alambrista. Dir. Robert M. Young. Filmhaus, 1977. DVD.

Bakhtin, Mikhail M. (1981) *Dialogic Imagination: Four Essays.* Austin: U of Texas P.

Boriboj. (2009). *Cary Fukunaga Sin Nombre interview Karlovy Vary* [Video file]. Web: https://youtu.be/zF7QdLl4PRM?list=PLh3ihWGCrVWZ8EJ xzxWx1IccxDWzeNWls.

CorreCamara. (2014) *Entrevista con Luis Mandoki para CorreCamara parte 1 de 2* [Video file]. Web: https://youtu.be/h_uwVzeEt48.

Crusellas, Quim. (2007) *EL CINEMATÒGRAF "VOCES INOCENTES* [Video file]. Web: https://youtu.be/VPPQuyzYaVE?list= PLh3ihWGCrVWZ8EJxzxWx1IccxDWzeNWls.

Diaz, Tom. (2009) *No Boundaries: Transnational Latino Gangs and American Law Enforcement.* Ann Arbor: U of Michigan.

Domínguez-Ruvalcaba, Héctor and Corona, Ignacio. (2010) *Gendered Violence at the U.S.-Mexico Border: Media Representation and Public Response.* Tucson: The U of Arizona.

Fountain, John W. (2002) "Skeletons Tell Tale of Gamble by Immigrants." *The New York Times.*

Fregoso, Rosa Linda (1993) *The Bronze Screen: Chicana and Chicano Film Culture.* Minneapolis: U of Minnesota P.

---. (2003) *meXicana encounters: The Making of Social Identities on the Borderlands.* Barkley: U of California P.

Gonzalez-Barrera, Ana, Krogstad, Jens Manuel. (2014) "Number of Latino Children Caught Trying to Enter U.S. Nearly Doubles in Less Than a Year." Washington DC: Pew Research Center.

Gonzalez, Juan. (2000) *Harvest of Empire: A History of Latinos in America.* New York City: Viking Press.

Lee, Erika. (1998) *At America's Gates: Chinese Immigration During the Exclusion Era, 1882-1943.* Chapel Hill: The University of North Carolina Press.

Maciel, David R. (1990) *El Norte: The U.S.-Mexican Border in Contemporary Cinema.* San Diego: San Diego State University.

MovieCollege. (2010) Interview by Cary Fukunaga 'Sin Nombre' [Video file]. Web: https://youtu.be/bId-

YNWjiek?list=PLh3ihWGCrVWZ8EJ
xzxWx1IccxDWzeNWls.

Nazario, Sonia. (2006) *La Travesía de Enrique*. New York: Random House Paperbacks.

Ngai, Mae M. (2014) *Impossible Subjects: Illegal Aliens and the Making of Modern America*. Princeton: Princeton University Press.

Noriega, Chon A. (1991) *Road to Aztlán: Chicanos and Narrative Cinema*. Stanford: University Microfilms International. A Bell & Howell Company.

---. (1992) *Chicanos and Film: Essays on Chicano Representation and Resistance*. Garland Publishing, Inc.

---. (2000) *Shot in America: Television, the State, and the Rise of Chicano Cinema*. Minneapolis: U of Minnesota P.

Paredes, Americo. (1995) *A Texas-Mexican Cancionero: Folksongs of the Lower Border*. Austin, TX, USA: University of Texas Press, Reprint Edition.

Pegler-Gordon, Anna. (2009) *In Sight of America: Photography and the Development of U.S. Immigration Policy*. Oakland: University of California Press.

Saldívar, José David. (2011) *Trans-Americanity: Subaltern Modernities, Global Coloniality, and the Cultures of Greater Mexico*. Durham: Duke University Press.

Schmidt-Camacho, Alicia. (2008) *Migrant Imaginaries: Latino Cultural Politics in the U.S.-Mexico Borderlands*. New York: New York UP.

Sin Nombre. Dir. Cary Joji Fukunaga. Focus Features, 2009. DVD.

Staudt, Kathleen. (2008) *Violence and Activism at the Border: Gender, Fear, and Everyday Life in Ciudad Juárez*. Austin: U of Texas P.

Staudt, Kathleen, Payan, Tony, and Kruszewski, Anthony Z. (2009) *Human Rights along the U.S. Mexico Border: Gendered Violence and Insecurity*. Tucson: The U of Arizona P.

Torres, Oscar. "The Making of Voces Inocentes." Public Lecture at University of California at Santa Barbara, Santa Barbara, CA, Feb. 09, 2011.

Voces Inocentes. Dir. Luis Mandoki. 20th Century Fox, 2004. DVD.

ZOLTÁN PETERECZ

THE QUESTION OF AMERICAN EXCEPTIONALISM AT THE TIME OF THE MEXICAN-AMERICAN WAR

A recent Gallup poll showed that a huge majority of Americans (80%) agreed with the following statement: "the United States has a unique character because of its history and Constitution that sets it apart from other nations as the greatest in the world." When asked whether the United States has "a special responsibility to be the leading nation in world affairs," two-thirds of the respondents gave a positive answer (Jones 2010). Although not termed in the well-known expression, the results of this questionnaire prove that the large majority of the United States still subscribes to the notion of American exceptionalism. The overwhelming majority still clings to the "city on the hill" metaphor as the underlying justification for the United States as beacon to the free world, as an example to behold. Despite the polling, one may still find cause to debate about just what American exceptionalism really is. Whether it is one concept; or a series of idea(l)s about the United States, or just a bunch of self-gratifying myths upon which to ground one's system of belief (for the origin of the term see Ceaser 2012, 1-26).

Since the birth of the United States, but indeed, from the very first years of the English colonization of the North American continent, the origins of what is now collectively called American exceptionalism can be detected. How should one define this notion, which today sometimes finds itself in the danger of being trite and overused? This phenomenon has a narrower and a broader interpretation. As one scholar puts it, it is "the notion that the United States has had a unique destiny and history, or more modestly, a history with high distinctive features or an unusual trajectory" (Kammen 1993, 6). As another observer put it, "America marches to a different drummer. Its uniqueness is explained by any or all of a variety of reasons: history, size, geography, political institutions, and culture" (Rose 1989, 91-115). According to Ian Tyrell, the concept has three main pillars that rest upon religious, political, and material or economic concerns (Tyrrell 2013). There is a general American belief that articulates that this nation has a larger-than-life role in shaping the form of the world because it possesses a special status as God's chosen nation and is exempt, to a large degree, from the laws of history.

At any rate, it can be safely asserted that the notion of chosenness, being an example to the rest of the world, and some form of mission coming from the previous tenets are part of what one might label American exceptionalism. Everybody agrees on one important thing: American exceptionalism is part of the national identity of the United States, a self-sustaining myth that refuses to lie down. It can be stated with a large measure of confidence that the concept entails that this new country, with its new form of government, was a God-sent "gift" to mankind, and exactly this is why there is the "mission" component of American exceptionalism. In this reading it is not enough to shine as the bright example to follow; the United States has a providential mission. This is nothing less than to spread freedom all over the world.

Most adherents of American exceptionalism connect the idea of mission to John Winthrop and his famous sermon delivered upon his arrival in the New World in 1630. His "city upon a hill" image is much ingrained, and identified, with the United States, at least on one level of explanation. The Puritan community indeed wished to serve as an example to others to follow, because if they did not live up to the wishes of God, they would become in Winthrop's opinion "a story and a by-word through the world" (Winthrop 1630. A more detailed analysis about Winthrop's thoughts and the declaration in question see, Gamble 2012; Litke 2010, 54-104). Ten years later Peter Bulkeley echoed Winthrop but also surpassed him, when he said, "Thou shouldst be a special people, an only people, none like thee in all the earth" (Bulkeley 1653, 16). Naturally, one cannot speak about Americans when one mentions the Puritans, but it is an undeniable fact that the Puritan heritage can be detected in modern-day United States. A century later Jonathan Edwards believed and preached that the people on the eastern shores of the continent were to be "the glorious renovator of the world" (qtd. in Rossiter 1950-51, 21). It is important to mention, however, that Virginians thought of themselves just as chosen by God as their fellow settlers to the north had come to believe. John Rolfe, for example, was equally certain that the migration from England to Virginia was characteristic of "a *peculiar people* marked and chosen by the *finger* of God" (Rolfe 1617/1951, 41; emphasis in the original). The point is that the idea of being chosen can be found as early as the first English settlers made their way into the new continent, which they often described as "the wilderness." They established the germ of a myth that would live on and gain ever more strength throughout the centuries.

When the roughly two and a half million former British colonists in North America had gained their independence from the mother country, and had chosen to become a new nation, Americans, they began the great experiment of forming a republican state with a pluralist democratic system. In the ratification debate of the Constitution of 1787, the propaganda tool of the Federalists, Alexander Hamilton, James Madison, and John Jay's essays in the *Federalist Papers*, aside from their thorough examination of the advantages of the new constitution, also claimed the virtues of the document to an abnormally high degree. These otherwise quite realistic persons said of the Constitution that "Happy will it be for ourselves, and most honorable for human nature, if we have wisdom and virtue enough, to set so glorious an example to mankind!" (Hamilton, 1788, Federalist No. 36, 175). It would be too simplistic, however, to label such rhetorical phenomenon as this, and the many coming before and after them, only propaganda. To be sure, some of it was nothing more than political advertising. But to a large extent, perhaps partly due to the propaganda itself, this has become part of the American DNA, an unquestionable truth about the character and goal of the nation.

The young nation's first president, George Washington, claimed that "Every step by which they have advanced to the character of an independent nation seems to have been distinguished by some token of providential agency." Here, in Washington's rhetoric such a line of thought is expressed that has always been there, before and since winning independence from Great Britain, that "the preservation of the sacred fire of liberty and the destiny of the republican model of government are justly considered, perhaps, as deeply, as finally, staked on the experiment entrusted to the hands of the American people" (Hunt 2003, 6). Washington thus set another of his many precedents that served as guidance to his nation. And followers abounded. Thomas Jefferson subscribed to his metaphor based on the laws of motion in which he prophesied about the expansion of freedom following the American path: "This ball of liberty, I believe most piously, is now so well in motion that it will roll around the globe" (Leicester 1892-99, 22). In his first official communication as president he also set the rhetorical milestone picked up by many of his future followers: "this Government, the world's best hope" (Hunt 2003, 25). Only two days later he gave proof for the exemplary strain of the American mission as well, when he wrote to another Founding Father that "a just and solid republican government maintained here, will be a standing monument and example for the aim and imitation of the people of other countries" (Fried 1963, 407). A year later he wrote that "We feel that we are acting under obligations not confined to the limits of our own society. It is impossible not to be sensible that we are acting for all mankind" (Rossiter 1950-51, 22). He was also the one who moved from "empire of liberty" to "empire for liberty," a significant change in meaning, and hardly an accidental slip of tongue. And by acquiring the Louisiana

Territory from Napoleon in 1803, Jefferson did everything in his power to bring that transition closer to reality. Andrew Jackson in his farewell address also left an indelible mark on the mission component: "Providence has showered on this favored land blessings without number, and has chosen you as the guardians of freedom, to preserve it for the benefit of the human race" (Peters and Woolley).

What might be labeled aggressive exceptionalism can be dated to the time of the Monroe Doctrine. This unilateral foreign policy declaration warned the European powers to stay away from the Americas, especially from Latin America, because the ruling political form was democratic, that is, these countries were trying to follow the American example. Any thought or action concerning the recolonization of Latin America by Spain or another European power would be seen as a national security threat to the United States to which adequate answers would be given. This somewhat brazen announcement was based on shrewd recognition of geopolitical facts and possibilities, and with time it ensured a free hand to the US government with respect to intra-American affairs. One must not lose sight of the balancing act of the principal author behind the Monroe Doctrine: John Quincy Adams. Adams, then Secretary of State, had two years earlier confirmed that the United States would not go abroad, "in search of monsters," rather he declared America must pursue a passive foreign policy vis-à-vis Europe, and freedom must find a way there, or elsewhere, without American military help (*Niles' Weekly Register* 1821, 331). Realism always kept a check on idealism (on the tension between the idealist and realist camps in the United States on how foreign policy course should be followed, see Graebner 2002, 311-328). Monroe's doctrine came to serve American interests, present and future alike, in immeasurable ways. As the eminent historian, Samuel Flagg, observed, "it was inseparable from the continental expansion of the United States. It was a voice of Manifest Destiny" (qtd. in Bemis 1949, 407).

As the ideology of Manifest Destiny grew, so too grew the realization of American exceptionalism. Both ideas entailed an aggressive mode of thinking, since westward expansion was encoded in rhetoric and speech making of the era (on the topic of Manifest Destiny see Weinberg 1935; Merk 1963; Graebner 1968; Heidler 2003). This thought, claiming that it was the United States' God-ordained future to reach the Pacific Ocean and inhabit all of the continental land, proved to be the central motive for the expansion of the nation in the first half of the nineteenth century. One historian summed up this notion as

> embracing all the ideas hitherto considered—geographical determinism, the superiority of democratic institutions, the superior fecundity, stamina, and ability of the white race—became a justification for almost any

34

addition of territory which the United States had the will and the power
to obtain (Pratt, 1935 345).

Another group of historians defined Manifest Destiny as "a justification
of imperialism in terms of American exceptionalism" (Citrin 1994, 23).
Either way, the frontier, which had been an integral part of life of the
settlers from the earliest days, was moving westward.

Frontier, in the European sense, has a much more clearly defined
meaning than in the American usage. For centuries, European nations and
their forerunners have been used to living in well-defined spaces. In
Europe, the frontier is a borderline on the map which is not to be crossed
or trouble is invited. It is what the historian Walter Prescott Webb termed
"the sharp edge of sovereignty" (Webb 1952, 2). Under the circumstances
of the North American continent, the British colonists-turned-Americans
had a different attitude toward the frontier. Webb argues that

> the American thinks of the frontier as lying *within*, and not at the edge of
> a country. It is not a line to stop at, but an *area* inviting entrance. Instead
> of having one dimension, length, as in Europe, the American frontier has
> two dimensions, length and breadth. In Europe the frontier is stationary
> and presumably permanent; in America it *was* transient and temporal
> (Webb 1952, 2-3).

It is a logical step forward that the frontier was "the idea of a body of
free land which can be had for the taking" (Webb 1952, 3). From this the
concept of possible expansion was imbedded in the Americans, who
thought the land was free and belonged to those who took it.

The pioneer and godfather of Manifest Destiny was John O'Sullivan and
his various articles in the *Democratic Review*, an influential media outlet of the
day. He preached that the United States "must onward to the fulfillment of
our mission." O'Sullivan declared that the integral elements of expansion
were "freedom of conscience, freedom of person, freedom of trade and
business pursuits, universality of freedom and equality" (O'Sullivan 1839,
430). Moreover, he wrote the United States had been chosen for the high
purpose of establishing "the moral dignity and salvation of man." In a few
years' time O'Sullivan had managed to pursue much of the nation of the
correct tenets of his views, and Manifest Destiny had overtaken almost the
entire view of the nation. In his essay titled "Annexation," he vehemently
argued for the annexation of Texas and called on the U.S. to bring the
region into its rightful place within the Union. Employing a rather
circumspect determinism, O'Sullivan saw benevolence in American
expansionism; his was a clear-cut sense that taking Texas was justified as a
moral mission (O'Sullivan 1845, 17).

Since its declaration of independence in 1836, Texas was a coveted piece of land for the Union, and vice versa. This was not only about expansion alone, but it bore a real significance on international affairs. It was no secret that Europeans powers, mainly Great Britain, toyed with the idea of recognizing Texas as an independent country as counterbalance to the growing United States. Taking into account of the highly sensitive threat perception of the United States, it is little wonder that they annexed the huge territory into the Union in 1845. This was a step that made almost inevitable that there would be armed conflict with Mexico. Not only had Texas been taken from Mexico, there was also California in the possession of Mexico, another valuable continental real estate that the growing United States wished to possess. Just a few weeks before a declaration of war against Mexico was made by Congress William Gilpin issued a report to the Senate. Gilpin was partly responsible for fueling "Oregon fever" by spreading the semi-mythical accounts of acquisition of the western lands that were larded with American nationalistic sentiment. Similarly, in addressing the Senate he argued to convince political decision makers:

> The *untransacted* destiny of the American people is to subdue the continent—to rush over this vast field to the Pacific Ocean—to animate the many hundred millions of its people, and to cheer them upward—to set the principle of self-government at work—to agitate these herculean masses—to establish a new order in human affairs—to set free the enslaved—to regenerate superannuated nations—to change darkness into light—to stir up the sleep of a hundred centuries—to teach old nations a new civilization—to confirm the destiny of the human race—to carry the career of mankind to its culminating point—to cause stagnant people to be re-born—to perfect science—to emblazon history with the conquest of peace—to shed a new and resplendent glory upon mankind—to unite the world in one social family—to dissolve the spell of tyranny and exalt charity —to absolve the curse that weighs down humanity, and to shed blessings round the world! *Divine task! immortal mission* ! Let us tread fast and joyfully the open trail before us! Let every American heart open wide for patriotism to glow undimmed, and confide with religious faith in the sublime and prodigious destiny of his well-loved country (Gilpin 1873, 124).

It is easy to see that the text spews militant force ("subdue," "rush over," "regenerate," "teach," "confirm", "cause," or "emblazon"), all reinforcing Gilpin's missionary zeal. As it turned out there was more to Gilpin than talk and he became a combatant at the start of the Mexican War. Gilpin was just one of many trumpeting the clarion call of expansion in the guise of liberty and American uniqueness. Senator and later President James Buchanan declared in March 1844: "Providence has given to the American people a great and important mission, and that mission they were destined to fulfill—to spread the blessings of Christian liberty and laws from one end to the other of this immense continent." And, in his view, to restrain American expansion on the continent was "like talking of limiting the stars in their courses, or bridling the foaming torrent of Niagara" (qtd. in Graebner 1985, 185). Another Congressman was more succinct: "We received our rights from high Heaven, from destiny, if you please" (qtd. in Graebner 1985, 199).

Despite such rallying campaign calls as "54'40" or fight," the United States being aware that it did not wish to confront British military might was trying to avoid any possible clashes with Britain over the Oregon Territory. Another consideration was the tacit alliance between the U.S. and England where in terms of the geopolitical goals the two countries in many cases agreed. Still emotions could run high concerning Oregon. In this quarrelsome matter James Buchanan affirmed in Congress that Providence had provided Americans with the mission of "extending the blessings of Christianity and of civil and religious liberty over the whole North American continent" (Pratt 1935, 342). A senator from Illinois called the hopeful extension into the whole of Oregon territory "a desire only to extend more widely the area of human freedom" (qtd. in Pratt 1935, 342). Still realism, a constant check on idealist American stirring, proved supreme once again. The flexing muscle of the nascent American empire was looking to weaker opponents, and Mexico offered the ripest example for a showdown.

The question of Oregon was closely related to that of Mexico. In Texas more and more Americans were coming to settle and their taxes were welcomed by the Mexican government. Within time, however, the growing number of Americans began showing dislike toward the centralist government in Mexico City and worked openly to join the United States as a new member state. The end result of that tension was a short local war, which ended with an independent Texas in 1836. After Texas gained its independence and successfully sought annexation to the Union, it was just a matter of time before the two antagonistic nations squared off against each other. Mexican honor fueled a desperate attempt to hold on to a vast, northern expanse of territory, while American expansionist fever could not be satisfied until reaching the Pacific and conquering the lands in-between.

Here was the opportunity of a spectacular show of force in the name of American pride, American virtue, and American nationalism—collectively subsumed under the notion of American exceptionalism. Those who favored a masculine consideration of American exceptionalism deeply believed that the American example must be spread. The various tribes, nations, and countries were simply on a lower level of civilization than the United States, or so they argued. American exceptionalism came to mean the conquest of Indian tribes and Mexicans; it was the way to advance freedom; a way to promote equality; a way to further God's will—and this belief justified the use of war and military force. Adherents of American exceptionalism were convinced that everyone would benefit in the long run. But Mexico stood in the way of the spread of such rewards. Its presence in the West ran counter to American ambitions, and since it did not understand what Americans thought was the superior force of historical tides, the United States' military might had to act. Nothing and no one could stand in the way of marching progress on the North American continent.

At this junction it was impossible to avert a war with Mexico. The French observer, Alexis de Tocqueville, a few years earlier had already predicted such an outcome. "The boundaries between these two races have been fixed by a treaty. But however favorable that treaty may have been to the Anglo-Americans, I have no doubt that they will soon infringe it" (Tocqueville 2000, 409). With a realistic assessment of reigning power relations on the North American continent, the perspicacious Frenchman rightfully added, "it must not be thought possible to halt the impetus of the English race in the New World" (Tocqueville 2000, 411). In May, 1846, the United States declared War on Mexico and started a military campaign against a weak foe that could not resist the more powerful and modern army of the United States.

The favorable outcome of the war waged against Mexico in 1846-1848 gave the citizens of the U.S. a perfect reason to yet again engage in open debate about American exceptionalism, Manifest Destiny, and the role of the United States in the world. An inevitable clash between the two opposing camps took place. Both groups argued according to their own interpretation of American exceptionalism. Victory over Mexico provided a unique way to measure what many thought the mission of the nation was, what the message of God to the American nation really meant, and what shape exemplary behavior indeed had to take. What is more important, however, for a long time to come it was decided which side was more influential and came out victorious. American society was just as divided as the political elite. On the one hand, the hope of another huge territorial gain gratified many citizens. On the other hand, it was easy to detect that such a further growth of land (nobody really toyed with the idea that Mexico could win) would intensify certain domestic political issues, first and foremost that of slavery.

U.S. President, James Knox Polk, a hardline expansionist, naturally shared the vision of Manifest Destiny, and believed that the war with Mexico was another act in the historical play penned by God. In his inaugural address he insisted that the United States was the "most admirable and wisest system of well-regulated self-government among men ever devised by human minds," it was obvious that the spread of such a system entailed positive results to those affected by it (Hunt, 1997 142). Those who raised their voice against this magnificent and God-ordained mission, let alone acts committed against it, "would extinguish the fire of liberty, which warms and animates the hearts of happy millions and invites all the nations of the earth to imitate our example" (Hunt 1987, 143-144). Naturally, Polk was a realistic diplomat and understood the relationship of power between nations. This gave only further impetus to his view that his country stood for "a model and example of free government to all the world," as well as "the star of hope and haven of rest to the oppressed of every clime" (qtd. in Nagel, 1964, 152). In his annual message in 1846, Polk declared, "The progress of our country in her career of greatness, not only in the vast extension of our territorial limits, and the rapid increase of our population, but in resources and wealth, and in the happy condition of our people, is without an example in the history of nations" (Polk 1846). Not surprisingly, Robert J. Walker, Polk's Secretary of the Treasury, shared this view. To him, the history of his nation amply testified "that a higher than earthly power still guards and directs our destiny, impels us onward, and has selected our great and happy country as a model and ultimate center of attraction for all the nations of the world" (qtd. in Nagel 1964, 152). The example as the apparent feature of American exceptionalism is hard to miss, and because Mexico said "no" to such a mission underwritten by God, the United States, the argument went, was left with no other choice but war. In other words, a country defending its sovereignty had to bow before the might of the sword that was taken out of the sheath of ideology.

Various representatives of the people in Congress also echoed the seemingly sweeping sentiment, right before and during the war, as to how important it was to spread liberty to not so long ago distant lands. As one Congressman put it, "Let us expand to our true and proper dimensions, and our liberty will be eternal; for, in the process, it will increase in strength, and the flame grow brighter, whilst it lights a more extensive field" (qtd. in Graebner 1968, 218). Passivity, in this reading, was detrimental to both the national and universal mission, because to "set bounds to the indomitable energy of our noble race...would be treason to the cause of human liberty" (Hunt 1987, 31; Hunt gives a concise overview of the debate raging in the first half of the nineteenth century concerning the American mission and its foreign policy manifestation so see also Hunt, 1987, 29-36). Another representative, while defending Polk's action concerning the war, called the Mexicans a "half-civilized people," emphasizing the prevailing racial thinking (Haralson 1846, 4). Bedinger from Virginia well summarized the opinion of the Democratic Party and its followers when he said on the floor of the House of Representatives that "the sympathy of the American people for the cause of freedom is beyond all control." He hoped it would be "nothing but a war of conquest," the purpose of which was manifold:

"an honorable peace," "teaching a barbarous people how to regard the laws of nations," "teaching demi-savages the rules of civilization, of decency, and common courtesy," and, finally, "letting the world see that we know how we to preserve and defend our rights and our sacred honor" (Bedinger 1847, 5-6). A Louisiana representative, even in his fervent defense of Southern slavery, he managed to argue:

> We, the United States, are the beacon light to the world. The advancement of this government in power, is the advancement of the liberty of mankind… For if this mighty fabric falls [the United States half slave, half free], the great hope of man for freedom will be crushed for centuries under the iron heel of despotism.

After these initial thoughts came the grand finish whose echoes were long heard later in the history of the United States:

> Let our Union progress in its mission. Let it stretch its arms to the Pacific, and control the commerce of that ocean. It will give us riches, and power to spread our religion and civilization to the barbarous and benighted pagans of Asia. Let the now well-nigh desert waste between the Mississippi and the Pacific, be filled up by us and our children. Let our agricultural States, both slaveholding and non-slaveholding, wheel into our great national army on its march to a more perfect civilization, and break down all obstacles to our intercourse with the world. If so, fifty years will not elapse, ere the destines of the human race will be in our hands. May God, in his infinite wisdom direct that power, when lodged with us, to the security of virtue, happiness, and freedom to man. (Harmanson 1847, 12-14)

Not all Americans agreed with the view of President Polk and his political allies and followers, however. A sizeable group of people, thinkers, politicians, part of the same elite that was so fervently for war, disagreed about the path to be taken by the country. They wished to see restraint instead of zeal. These people thought American exceptionalism meant modesty, avoiding expansion by conquering others, and conducting a truly virtuous domestic and foreign policy. Many were afraid of the further spread of slavery in the soon-to-be acquired territory. This was important because the thorny question of slavery not simply divided North and South, but had already started to loosen the basic structure of the Union. This line of thinking was most typical of the Whig Party. Former Secretary of State Henry Clay, for example, who was one of the most eminent politicians at the time, opposed the war with Mexico. He reasoned that "we should keep our lamp burning brightly on this western shore as a light to all nations, than to hazard its utter extinction amid the ruins of fallen or falling republics of Europe" (qtd. in Hay 1991, 945-946). Clay's view was essentially that of a pacifist but this did not mean, however, that he did not share the concept of the special status of his country in the world. In a Senate speech in 1839 he spoke of a "bright and effulgent and cheering light that beams all around us" that was capable of eliminating dark spots far away. Then he posed the question: did any other nation "ever contain within its bosom so many elements of prosperity, of greatness, and of glory?" (Bancroft 1855, 434). Others in Congress spoke of American exceptionalism as a highly questionable path to follow, at least in the shape of a war of conquest. One Congressman from Vermont used harsh words in his opposition to Polk and his political faction:

> This principle of a nation extending the blessings of its own institutions by *force and conquest*, has always, and in all ages, been the banes of nations... This plea of *destiny* has, among all bad men, in all past time, been only the weak and disgraceful apology for crime. It is the convicted *felon* only who apologizes for crime, by insisting that it was his *destiny*; and he is rightly *destined to disgrace* (Collamer 1848, 13; emphasis in the original).

A New York Whig also questioned the exceptionalist sentiment at large:

> Away with this wretched cant about a 'manifest destiny,' a 'divine mission,' a warrant from the Most High, to civilize, and christianize, and democratize our sister republics at the mouth of the cannon; sentiments which have found their way from dinner-table toasts and 'Empire club' harangues, to the mouths of grave Senators, and even, I have heard, to the public itself (Duer 1848, 13).

A major figure of the era was John C. Calhoun of South Carolina, who had occupied every important national office except for the presidency. Although his rhetoric helped the coming of the Civil War, he was decidedly against the forceful expansion toward the West. Shortly before the conclusion of the war with Mexico he warned in the Senate that if it was "the mission of this country to spread civil and religious liberty over all the globe," by force if there was no other alternative, it was "a sad delusion" (Calhoun 1848, 12). He maintained that history had rarely provided, if at all, a constitutional government that was characterized by free government and endurance. "Foresight and wisdom" were rare commodities in history, he cautioned, because any such case was only "the result of a fortunate combination of circumstances" (13). He was appalled that the US Congress, and the country at large, was occupied with "military glory, extension of the empire, and the aggrandizement of the country" (Calhoun, 1848, 13). As he put it, to preserve it, it is indispensable to adopt a course of moderation and justice towards all other countries; to avoid war whenever it can be avoided; to let those great causes which are now at work, and which, by the mere operation of time, will raise our country to an elevation and influence which no country has ever heretofore attained, continue to work. By pursuing such a course, we may succeed in combining greatness and liberty—the highest possible greatness with the largest measure of liberty—and do more to extend liberty by our example over this continent and the world generally, than would be done by a thousand victories (Calhoun, 1848, 14).

He was adamant that there was a more modest form of American exceptionalism. Or Albert Gallatin can be cited, who, as a believer of the original American exceptionalist creed, found fault with the expansionist sentiment. As he said, the American mission was to be

a model for all other governments and for all other less-favored nations, to adhere to the most elevated principles of political morality, to apply all your faculties to the gradual improvement of your own institutions and social state, and by your example to exert a moral influence most beneficial to mankind at large. But the war with Mexico brought nothing but "false glory" (Gallatin 1848, 14).

Still, the die was cast, and once the war was on, there was no looking back. The immense pressure of those who wanted to settle in the west (these years are also the first large wave of immigration, especially from Ireland, who were in search of free land), those who wished to see military glory, and those who earnestly believed in spreading freedom as an essential benefit to the human race, all joined in the war effort and that would lead to the conquering of the new territories. They wanted and would see the consummation of Manifest Destiny. By reaching the Pacific Coast Americans had fulfilled their hopes and destiny, they kept building their empire *of* and *for* freedom, they made sure that future Americans could enjoy the fruits of this expansion. Commodore Robert F. Stockton, a leading military figure in the takeover of California, verbalized the sentiment of a large segment of the nation at a dinner in Philadelphia in 1847: "We have a duty before God which we cannot—we must not evade. The priceless bond of civil and religious liberty has been confided to us as trustees" (qtd. in Graebner 1985, 249). Generations of Americans were influenced by these ideas through which their religion, their democratic institutions, their individualism, their civil rights and liberties, their national cohesion of the community, and their belief that the U.S. was a chosen nation, an example to the world. As the U.S. minister in London wrote, "it is our mission to extend commerce, the pioneer of civilization and child of peace to all parts of the world," and "to illustrate by our example the elevating effects of Christianity" (qtd. in Sexton 2011, 117).

Over time, the active, aggressive, wing of U.S. society got the upper hand and it was their definition of the national mission that was put in practice; it was their side of American exceptionalism that reigned supreme. And, as most generally happens with military successes, the war against Mexico framed the U.S. as an energetic, expansionist nation, whose energy, the logic went, would advance liberty, and not merely fuel only land hunger and military glory. Senator Stephen Douglas would remark, a "young nation with all her freshness, vigor, and youth desires no limits fixed to her greatness, no boundaries to her future growth" (qtd. in Carr 1909, 37). In his inaugural address in 1853, President Franklin Pierce set forth the metaphor of a light for freedom standing at the center of American progress: "The oppressed throughout the world from that day to the present have turned their eyes hitherward, not to find those lights extinguished or to fear lest they should wane, but to be constantly cheered by their steady and increasing radiance" (Hunt 1997, 165).

As a consequence of the war and signing of the Treaty of Guadalupe Hidalgo in February 1848, the United States gained a huge territory, almost 900,000 square miles, more than a quarter of present-day United States, not including Alaska. The vast and scarcely populated area opened up before subsequent waves of settlers, who transformed the region to a significant degree. New values, new laws, new customs and traditions were sprayed on these lands, under the tutelage of Americans. It should not and could not be argued that American exceptionalism was the only dividing line of argument at the time of the Mexican-American War. The important ports of the Pacific and their promise of further commercial activity with an eye on China and Japan was a major consideration in acquiring Upper California. The invariably nagging question of slavery, and the political demagoguery in which all this was wrapped, did also play an important and integral part of the whole historical picture. The Polk administration wanted to steer attention as well from the Oregon compromise, which was against a significant slice of those who got him in the White House. As what California is regarded, a quarter century prior to the war, a Congressional committee had already proposed the idea of settling the western shores of the North American continent. As the committee concluded, "by a little care and small expense, the citizens of this Republic might reap all the benefits of this trade [especially fur], not only profitable now, but... [to] increase for many years... The Committee cannot doubt that an establishment made on the Pacific... would give this country the advantage of all its own treasures, which otherwise must be lost forever, or rather never enjoyed" (qtd. in Bemis 1949, 487).

In the ensuing Congressional debate, the notion of what lay behind casting the Republic's eyes on the Pacific shore was well summarized by Francis Baylies of Massachusetts:

> Sir, our natural boundary is the Pacific Ocean. The swelling tide of our population must and will roll on until that mighty ocean interposes its waters, and limits our territorial empire. Then, with two oceans washing our shores, the commercial wealth of the world is ours, and imagination can hardly conceive the greatness, the grandeur, and the power that await us (qtd. in Bemis 1949, 513).

Although the Bill was not passed, it was an early and clearly indication of what lay ahead, a sentiment that with time gathered momentum. The San Francisco and San Diego Bays offered two magnificent natural harbors and various American business interests could not help but covet them with full force. The January 1846 issue of the *American Review* loudly claimed the privilege of the United States to gain the possession of California shortly before the war commenced. For the author of the article it was a place waiting to be elevated to a higher standard, by who else than Americans:

> no one who cherishes a faith in the wisdom of an overruling Providence, and who sees, in the national movements which convulse the world, the silent operation of an invisible but omnipotent hand, can believe it to be for the interest of humanity, for the well-being of the world, that this vast and magnificent region should continue forever in its present state (qtd. in Graebner 1985, 203).

Looking back, naturally it is easy to declare that the war with Mexico was partly an escape route form the trouble brewing among the North and South over slavery. Seemingly, the notion of aggressive American exceptionalism was the momentary safety valve from having to look in the mirror of the soul of the nation, and trying to decide peacefully about its future. For that, the bloodiest war in the history of the United States was needed. However, aside from the nagging question and further future problems of slavery, the United States happily marched on, with its eyes fixed on the horizon, ever ready to pounce on the chance to spread their cause of liberty, their values of "exceptional" nature, their belief in human progress, or to gain new territories, where all the preceding aspects could be exercised. The debate played out before and during the Mexican-American War of 1846-48 was in many ways just a prelude of later eerily identical debates. In this sense it is of even larger significance that the debate was decided in favor of those arguing for an active mode of American exceptionalism, an aggressive foreign policy course, paving the historical way for their future followers in the nineteenth, twentieth, and twenty-first centuries.

WORKS CITED

Bancroft, George. (1855) *Literary and Historical Miscellanies*. New York: Harper and Brothers.

Bedinger, Henry. (1847) Speech in Congress, January 6, 1847. Washington, D. C.: Blair and Rives, 1847.

Bemis, Samuel Flagg. (1949) *John Quincy Adams and the Foundations of American Foreign Policy*. New York: Alfred A. Knopf.

Bulkeley, Peter. (1653) *The Gospel-Covenant; Or, The Covenant of Grace Opened*, London: Matthew Simmons, 16.

Calhoun, John C. (1848) Speech in Congress, January 4, 1848. Washington, D. C.: John T. Towers.

Carr, Clark E. (1909) *Stephen A. Douglas: His Life, Public Services, Speeches and Patriotism*. Chicago: A. C. McClurg.

Ceaser, James W. (2012) "The Origins and Character of American Exceptionalism," *American Political Thought: A Journal of Ideas, Institutions, and Culture*, vol. 1 (Spring 2012), 1-26.

Citrin, Jack, Haas, Ernst B. Muste, Christopher, and Reingold, Beth. (1994) "Is American Nationalism Changing? Implications for Foreign Policy," *International Studies Quarterly*, Vol. 38, no. 1.

Collamer, Jacob. (1848) Speech in Congress, February 1, 1848. Washington, D. C.: J. & G. S. Gideon.

Duer, William. (1848) Speech in Congress, February 14, 1848. Washington, D. C.: J. & G. S. Gideon.

Ford, Paul Leicester, ed. (1892-99) *The Writings of Thomas Jefferson*, 10 vols. New York, 1892-99). vol. 7.

Fried, Albert, ed. (1963) *The Essential Jefferson* New York: Collier Books.

Gallatin, Albert. (1848) *Peace with Mexico*. Cincinnati: Daily Atlas Office.

Gamble, Richard M. (2012) *In Search of the City on a Hill. The making and Unmaking of an American Myth* New York, London: Continuum International Publishing Group.

Gilpin, William. (1873) *Mission of the North American People, Geographical, Social, and Political*. Philadelphia: J. B. Lippincott & Co.

Graebner, Norman A., ed (1968) *Manifest Destiny*. Indianapolis: Bobbs-Merrill.

Graebner, Norman A. (1985) *Foundations of American Foreign Policy: A Realist Appraisal from Franklin to McKinley*. Wilmington, Del.: Scholarly Resources, Inc.

Graebner, Norman A. (2002) "Realism and Idealism," In Richard D. Burns,. Alexander DeConde, and Frederik Logevall, eds., *Encyclopedia of American Foreign Policy* New York, NY: Scribner.

Hamilton, Alexander. (1788/1982) "Federalist No. 36: The Same Subject Continued (Concerning the General Power of Taxation)." In *The*

Federalist Papers by Alexander Hamilton, James Madison and John Jay. Edited and with an Introduction by Garry Wills, New York and Toronto: Bantam Books, 1982.

Haralson, Hugh A. (1846) Speech in Congress, July 16, 1846.Washington, D. C.: Blair and Rives.

Harmanson, John H. (1847) Speech, February 12, 1847.Washington, D. C.: Blair and Rives, 1847.

Hay, Melba Porter, ed. (1991) *The Papers of Henry Clay*, Vol. 10. Candidate, Compromiser, Elder Statesman, January 1, 1844-June 29, 1852. Lexington: The University Press of Kentucky, 1991.

Heidler, Davis S. and Jeanne T. Heidler (2003) *Manifest Destiny*. Westport, Connecticut, London: Greenwood Press.

Hunt, John Gabriel, ed. (1997) *The Inaugural Addresses of the Presidents*, New York: Gramercy Books.

Hunt, Michael H. (1987) *Ideology and U.S. Foreign Policy*. New Haven and London: Yale University Press.

Jones, Jeffrey M. (December 22, 2010) "Americans See U.S. as Exceptional; 37% Doubt Obama Does." Gallop Poll Report. Web: http://www.gallup.com/poll/145358/Americans-Exceptional-Doubt-Obama.aspx, accessed November 22, 2013

Kammen, Michael. (1993) "The Problem of American Exceptionalism: A Reconsideration," *American Quarterly*, *Vol.* 45, no. 1 (1993), 6.

Litke, Justin Blake. (2010) *American Exceptionalism: From Exemplar to Empire*. PhD dissertation, Washington, D.C.: Georgetown University.

Merk, Frederick. (1963) *Manifest Destiny and Mission in American History*. New York: Vintage Books.

Nagel, Paul C. (1964) *One Nation Indivisible. The Union of American Thought, 1776-1861*. Oxford University Press.

Niles' Weekly Register, 1821. No. 21, Vol. XX.

O'Sullivan, John L. (1839) "The Great Nation of Futurity", *The United States Democratic Review*, Vol. 6. No. 23.

O'Sullivan, John L. (1845) "Annexation," *The United States Magazine and Democratic Review*, Vol. 17.

Peters, Gerhard and Woolley, John T. *The American Presidency Project*. Web: http://www.presidency.ucsb.edu/ws/?pid=67087

Pratt, Julius. (1935) "The Ideology of American Expansion." In Avery Craven, ed., *Essays in Honor of William E. Dodd*. Chicago: University Of Chicago Press.

Rolfe, John. (1617) *A True Relation of the State of Virginia Lefte by Sir Thomas Dale Knight, in May Last 1616*, New Haven, CT: Yale University Press, 1951.

Rose, Richard. (1989) "How Exceptional is the American Political Economy?" *Political Science Quarterly* (1989) 104.1: 91-115.

Rossiter, Clinton. (1950-51) "The American Mission," *The American Scholar*, Vol. 20, no. 1, Winter 1950-51: 21.

Sexton, Jay. (2011) *The Monroe Doctrine. Empire and Nation in Nineteenth-Century America.* New York: Hill and Wang.

Tocqueville, Alexis de. (2000) *Democracy in America*, J. P. Mayer, ed., New York: Perennial Classics.

Tyrrell, Ian. (2013) "The Myth(s) That Will Not Die: American National Exceptionalism," in Gérard Bouchard, ed., *Constructed Pasts, Contested Presents* New York: Routledge.

Webb, Walter Prescott. (1952) *The Great Frontier.* Austin: University of Texas Press.

Weinberg, Albert Katz. (1935) *Manifest Destiny. A Study of Nationalist Expansionism in American History.* Baltimore: The Johns Hopkins Press.

Winthrop, John. (1630) "A Model of Christian Charity".

KITTI SOMOGYI

"THE CHILD WAS HIS WARRANT:" A JOURNEY FOR SURVIVAL IN CORMAC MCCARTHY'S *THE ROAD*

After the appalling events of 9/11, Americans lost their unflinching confidence and sense of security and became obsessed with a possible collapse of their current world order. A similar type of confidential crisis provided the frame for Cormac McCarthy's vision of a possible global destruction. In *The Road* (2006) the author set up a story about a father and his son placed into a barren, almost extinct, post-apocalyptic, frontier-type of America, where human relationships and moral values are destroyed. The two "pilgrims" (3) had to abandon their homeland after the catastrophe and headed to the South in search for a secure, warm place, escaping from "bad guys" (77). The father is dying while they move along, but he has an intention before he passes: to prepare the child for the day when he will be gone. Thus he teaches the boy how to sustain himself, to survive and remain moral and altogether human—under all circumstances.

Overall, McCarthy's novel negotiates between the historical and cultural status of the American frontier as such and a fictional global apocalypse that stands in contrast with two conceptions of historiography: the classical western history of the nineteenth century and that of the Progressive era, and the new western history elaborated in the 1980s by a newer generation of American historians. Frederick Jackson Turner's "The Significance of the Frontier in American History" (1893) emphasized the importance of the frontier in the advance in American history by highlighting Western America as the shaping force of the nation and national identity. As Clyde A. Milner II later claimed, the organizing principle for the creation of history was the "[s]ignificance for historical understanding, not the novelty of presentation" (xiii). With this statement Milner acknowledges Turner's thesis but also affirms a new western interpretation of Turner's vision when he writes that "Native Americans, Mexican Americans, and Asian Americans" as well as issues of "gender, the natural environment, human perception, and the role of the West itself in the nation's history" are not new topics at all to be discussed by a novel generation of western historians;

instead, it is "the significance of these topics" that is "new" (xiii). Furthermore, Michael Allen highlights the fact that Turner merely "expressed the beliefs of his own generation," while some of the new western historians, unfortunately continue to hold Turner's use of "imperialistic stereotypes" (206) in their essays. Apart from these, the most remarkable new western historian, Patricia Nelson Limerick, stresses in *The Legacy of Conquest: The Unbroken Past of the American West* (1987) that the process of historical creation of the frontier is a continuous process and not a closed episode, claiming that instead of progress, the "history of the West" is "a place undergoing conquest and never fully escaping its consequences" (26).

In his aforementioned novel, McCarthy developed, in my reading, the thoughts of the old and the new western historians by showing that the ravaged world of *The Road* can be the reversal of those paradigms that were the core of these historical ideas in focusing on the regress of the early twenty-first century American society in the wake of an unknown worldwide catastrophe. The first point in this regard is the survivors' migration towards South and the change from the fruitful progress of a prosperous country into a land of deprivation and global destruction; all seen through some kind of counter-frontier paradigm. This paradigm is primarily discernable in the novel through all those people who are forced to leave their homes and their accustomed lives rooted in a consumerist welfare society. Their deracination is unavoidable by reason of the progressive annihilation of the world, the approach of the threatening cold winter and the menace of abhorrent, sanguinary "bloodcults" (16) that haunt the wider region.

Cormac McCarthy has a blunt vision about the prospective of mankind's lack of future. He does not mention the cause of a worldwide catastrophe but the reader is made aware of the fact that whatever happened this was the consequence of a combination of the environmental abuse, historical sins and the political arrogance of the past. Though the reader cannot be sure of the ways in which the world was sentenced to death, there are some hints in the novel that there were "balefires" (16), that "all was burnt to ash" (14); and it is almost certain, that "[t]he clocks stopped at 1:17" while "[A] long shear of light and then a series of low concussions" occurred with the a "dull rose glow in the windowglass" (52). McCarthy does not specify it but is implied in the context that it might have been an environmental disaster that lead to this apocalyptic world. Paradoxically, the carelessness of humans toward nature goes back to the ages of the Westward expansion, when there were seemingly unlimited natural resources in the area. The most important asset was the vast "free land" (Turner 32) leading to various opportunities for the pursuit of happiness, personal wealth and great potential for economic progress. In

Turner's view, the progress in America was due to the Westward expansion, which started with the gradual conquest of nature. Later on, Patricia Limerick shared this idea and wrote that with the occupation of the West, "Americans continued to try to conquer nature, transforming a variety of resources into profitable commodities" (153). In order to reach higher profits and to make the most of the region's nature, they exploited the land until it became overused.

In the Western area of the U.S. there were vast areas of fertile soil used for growing wheat, and providing grazing-ground for raising animals; moreover, rivers, timber and minerals were supplying livelihood for the pioneers who were expecting instant prosperity. This rich, idyllic picture of the "Great West" (Turner 3) gradually turned into a disillusioning, burnt and desolated land in the novel set in the twenty-first century. McCarthy's heroes turn into less lucky people because they have to procure food, set up shelters and keep their children secure without promising them a future in a "[b]arren, silent, godless" (4) country. This "new world" offers little to both the father and the son, so the parent can only give essential knowledge, like setting a fire for warmth, or how to find a safe refuge for the night. The intention of the apocalyptic migrants' journey Southward differs from those of the "self-made men" of earlier times, who became mavericks for adventure's sake and in order to reach a higher social class through hard work—or simply good luck; the unnamed man (an Everyman in all senses of the word) and his son do not aim to be rich but only follow their faith, live nomadic lives and keep "carrying the fire" (83), striving to remain "good."

The frontier used to be the dream of the pioneers (with agriculture as the primary source of living) but unlike the ideological environment of the 'older' frontier, the landscape of *The Road* is completely infertile: everything is covered with ash, waters are filthy, and animals are all dead. Though the forefathers could make the most of the given land, those people who survived the catastrophe do not have the opportunity to produce anything. Their world became desert and people who used to live in neighborhoods became refugees unable to settle down any more anywhere; they cannot stay in one place for a long time because they have to flee from the "bad guys" (77) and the threatening cold aiming to reach the Pacific coast. Furthermore, there is "[s]o little of promise in that country" (88) where the fields are dead, and the soil is lixiviated by ash, the "old crops [are] dead and flattened" (21) while "[t]he alien sun commencing its cold transit" (178) scorches over their heads. In other words, the core of life is dead and nothing can bring it back again: the abundance of the frontier has turned into an apocalyptic counter-frontier. To some extent it is still a 'frontier' because there is wilderness and unknown land for the pioneers/survivors but the 'counter' attribute is that there is no fruitful land, no exploitable natural resources, no outlook for progress, and no potential in the place at all.

McCarthy created a world "shrinking down about a raw core of parsible entities" (88) degrading the former one onto separate, elemental pieces. The novelist's world is falling apart into nothingness, best illustrated with the falling trees that are burnt, rotten and "dead to the root" (21). Trees used to be shelter for birds and animals, stock for building houses, but were also used as levers for children's swinging or for lighting a fire to warm by. The tree as a symbol also represents life, and as such, human life, and when the man says to his child that "[a]ll the trees in the world are going to fall sooner or later" (35), his words imply the inevitability of death of all organic beings including animals and humans as well. Besides the tree, the symbol of the nineteenth century progress, the railroad, is also present in the novel: the father and his son come across a locomotive in the woods, which stands there abandoned, subserviced for a long time, a machinery that is "slowly decomposing for all eternity" (180). Trains and railroads used to be the connection between the American East and West, the first permanent, man-made link between Turnerian dichotomy of 'civilization' and 'savagery.' The first Transcontinental Railroad "pioneered the way for the pioneer" and, accordingly, Americanization started on the frontier with the railroads granting the "opportunity for economic and political fortunes" (Turner 104, 276, 145) and overall improvement. However, in *The Road* the railroad system is fading out showing the decay of the world.

With the westward expansion, the United States developed into one of the biggest nations and one of the greatest powers in the world. According to Turner, the US was "destined to be the greatest, the richest, the most prosperous of all the great, rich, and prosperous commonwealths which go to make up the mightiest republic the world has ever seen" (178). In *The Road*, Turner's conceptions of human supremacy over nature and other people, however, is deconstructed by hyperbolization. In order to show the essential deficiency of the apocalyptic world, human supremacy is represented by annihilation, emphasized by of the self-destructive effect of mankind's activities. Moreover, the American institutional democracy which— according to Turner—came into being by means of the frontier experience, to the attainment of complete freedom, becomes anarchy in *The Road*. In the destroyed (new) world in McCarthy's novel there is lawlessness, disorder, and chaos. The absence of political institutions, such as government, safety regulations or societal laws, leads to general turmoil. Starvation and deprivation bring danger and extreme violence—for example, cannibalism and the enslavement of good people by marauders. Thus the new world order reevaluates the Manichean conception between good and evil, similar to Turner's dichotomy of 'civilized' and 'savage' worlds. As a result, in the nineteenth century the frontier movement involved the emergence of new political and social institutions. Unknown circumstances evoked the intention in the pioneers to establish an unprecedented society without the legacy of the European standards, generating an American type of democracy. Vast, open, and plentiful fields meant a "fair, blank page" for pioneers "on which to write a new chapter in the story of man's struggle for a higher type of society" (Turner 261). With all its treasures, the frontier offered the stage for a new kind of alignment. Turner claimed, that "American democracy came from the forest, and its destiny drove it to material conquests" (154). With individual properties increasing, these required regulation, so democratic provisions were soon established in the West, too. New political institutions and legislation started to operate "with regard to land, tariff, and internal improvements" (Turner 154, 27) on the basis of frontier needs. In contrast with the emerging institutions of the growing country depicted by Turner, in McCarthy's narrative the shift from institutional democracy to unlimited anarchy forms the dominant shape of post-apocalyptic society. *The Road* describes in detail the ways in which humanity reached the stage of another type of 'freedom' through attendant lawlessness through which unwanted disorder rules every level of life by way of extreme violence and brutality. This process can be looked upon as an 'evolution backwards.' Regression is manifested in the meaningless journey of the survivors of the catastrophe, and the hopeless outlook to any kind of future they might have. While in the old West there was a potential to form democracy, the barren, dead fields in *The Road* trigger the opposite effect: there is no sense of settlement, development and or any human form of regulated life. Life in the anarchic new world is not only dangerous but can be easily fatal. Survivals of the global catastrophe live in "complete [but] purposeless freedom" (MacCurdy 347) in McCarthy's ravaged country. However, this freedom is not similar to the frontier age. The land, which used to appeal to American pioneers and all immigrants flooding these territories alike, is bereaved from its original, unperturbed state. In an anarchical state, in McCarthy's novel there are no restrictions, no limitations, so anyone can do whatever they wish or need. However, the most significant force that determines the deeds of all is the quest for food. The "lack of sustenance," as Carol MacCurdy writes, brings violence, terror, homicide and cannibalism (349). After marauders had looted not only abandoned houses but the whole country, with animals and plants dead, there is nothing left to eat. Most of the survivors choose degradation or suicide (as the protagonist child's mother) instead of starvation; some even resort to cannibalism, starting to eat "children in front of your eyes" (181) because of hunger.

Public safety in the West became important in the nineteenth century, mainly when people settled down and started to produce and accumulate goods. At the beginning, small communities kept order without any legal procedures or with local sheriffs. They had their own agreement that crime against one another was a larger affair than breaking any law (Limerick 62). As settled areas grew bigger and richer, more money and wealth was heaped; with the appearance of banks, the Western area became attractive for hell-raisers, bandits and thieves. The question of security became more important than ever in order to protect individual or public possessions and to secure civil safety. Enacting new laws and rights was therefore supplemented with highly improved defensive organs. In *The Road*, the threat of savagery, the fact of brutality and inhumanity is unimaginable. Blood cults live according to instincts and self-rule and practice authority by keeping others in permanent fear. The post-apocalyptic bandits create a wartime atmosphere as they are tramping along, armed with cold-steel, spears and lances. As McCarthy writes, "[b]ehind them came wagons drawn by slaves in harness and piled with goods of war and after that the women [...] some of them pregnant, and [...] consort of catamites illclothed against the cold and fitted in dogcollars and yoked each to each" (91-92). People are kept as slaves or rather edible animals by the side of the marching, self-appointed paramilitaries. This anachronistic picture is reminiscent of old wars when personal and civil rights were unacknowledged, and where the triumphant ones subdued the defeated.

Although the watchwords of the frontier movement were freedom, self-reliance, and development, along with the distinctive features of the new type of democracy entailing individual liberty, social mobility and the "well-being of the masses" (Turner 266), the most substantial matter of the new age in McCarthy's novel is existence "in a Darwinian world of survival of the fittest" (MacCurdy 348). With the end of the world, laws, rights, order, and every kind of system disappears, putting all human values into oblivion. The individual's survival in a world where life is sustainable only in solitude and distrust contrasts with the process of community building and nation formation of the pioneers in the nineteenth-century American West. Since all forms of community vanished after the apocalyptic events, McCarthy's novel questions the pragmatism behind the basic elements of American identity, among them the commitment to community and solidarity existent among frontier settlers. In the newly populated Western areas individuals, families, towns and larger associations required cooperation in order to manage their own interests. Later on the purpose of maintenance of property, safety and peace helped the unity of American peoples to join into a strong nation. According to Limerick, the West was the place capable to "force Americans out of their isolated, individualistic enterprises" putting them into "cooperation to build and maintain the necessary dams and ditches" and "[T]ransforming desert into garden" (136). In a somehow contradictory but still contingent way, both individualism and community building belonged to the main tenets of American identity. Taking a look at

The Road from the point of view of the communal spirit, the result is rankling: there are no countries any more, and there is neither need, nor opportunity for public groupings or a nation whatsoever. The only principle that remains is the isolation from the others during the journey each have to make in order to endure, and the most important purpose is to escape and to survive the cruelties of the new world—individually.

The two protagonists in the post-apocalyptic world go on the abandoned road together, being "each the other's world entire" (6), since they have neither relatives nor friends to rely on. The father raises the child alone among poor life conditions which he cannot change but he does his best to educate the boy's mind and spirit. He tells the child "[o]ld stories of courage and justice" (41), teaches him to play card games. However, those things are not enough for him to understand the old world because he only knows the standard of the new world that is full of hardship, fear, brutality—and dullness. Moreover, "[t]he child had his own fantasies. How things would be in the south. Other children" (54). The boy instinctively feels the need for a child-community. He dreams about the ways in which they will live after they reach the coast where they will find other good people. But reaching the seashore the child faces the truth: his expectations and dreams are proven unattainable. In place of the colorful cultures of the South, "where Indian America, Latin America, Anglo-America, Afro-America, and Asia" intersect (Limerick 27), there is just a dull, grey nothingness left. Losing his dreams of the South, the boy loses the meaning of life but his father encourages him to "keep trying" and not "give up" because that is what the "good guys" (137) do. The father's greatest fear, besides the cold weather, is the continuous lack of food. Whenever the boy asks his father to share what they have with others on the road, the father replies: "We can't share what we have or we'll die too" (52). They have to keep everything to themselves because they can hardly sustain their own lives. However, the well-educated child wants to help the poor and give food to an old man, Ely, and even to a thief, but especially to the child he thinks he saw in the town, saying: "I'd give that little boy half of my food" (86). He would like to share the life-keeping food with the "good guys" (77) because he wants to help others, making them into friends. In spite of the boy's generousness, the man forbids him to think about sharing their food, which would be an act against themselves. This situation resembles the hardships that the pioneers faced during their journey through the wilderness, when they were heading west. They did not have much food and in absence of drinking water, families or small groups of wanderers were divided in the question, with whom to share. As Limerick remarked, water "was a scarce resource as they crossed the deserts at the end of the journey. They had to make hard choices of loyalty, determining how much of their water to keep for their own survival and how much to share with their family and friends, and even with strangers in need (135).

Though the father has never been a criminal, the standard of the new world urges him to act offensively. Reaching the seashore they get robbed; all of their things, the tarp, the cart, their food are soon gone. They constantly starve and the father, sick for a long time, becomes weaker and more impatient against those who try to abuse them. Accordingly, they follow after the thief who robbed them and when they overtake him, the man takes proper revenge. The father takes all of the thief's belongings, saying angrily: "I'm going to leave you the way you left us" (257) and leaving a person dispossessed of his miserable life, but at the same time he saves his son from further starvation and imminent death. Later, the father explains to his son that their primal task is to take care of themselves and defend that little they have in order to stay alive.

Isolation from community and the migration across sullen, lifeless land is depressing and overwhelming to any survivor. As the man has lost his wife—and his whole world—the child is the new meaning of his life, showing him a new ray of light in the cold, dark world. The man reckons the little boy "his warrant" (5) who keeps him alive, and also calls him "the word of God" (5), who guides him on the road. McCarthy refers to the father's feeling stating that "the boy was all that stood between him and death" (29). Though they rarely speak, the father and his son are very close in spiritually. The closeness of the father and child relationship is revealed in gentle physical contacts such as the one when "[T]he boy held on to his hand" (26), and "clung to him crying, his head buried against his chest" (28). The father is the shelter for the little boy, one who represents security and protection. However, the man's inevitable death (MacCurdy 347) evokes fears in both of them; the father is scared of death because his son will remain alone and helpless in a tainted world. He is sleepless because of the perpetual questions: "Can you do it? When the time comes? Can you?" (29). The boy's greatest fear is losing his father, his leader, his savior and the only means to preserve his life. And when the man finally departs this life, the child mourns his father for three days. With the appearance of a strange man afterwards the little boy is frightened, yet he bravely faces him keeping his Papa's instruction in mind. The long-haired, strange man proves to be a "good guy" (282) after he answers several questions the boy asks him. It turns out that he has a family with two children, indicating that unlike others, who survived only individually, they have endured the hardships together. Joining a community is against the unwritten law of the new world standard, but this family proves to be the saving agency for the boy. The child has only two choices: to die alone or to accompany them. Keeping his father's words in his heart and knowing that he has to never give up, he chooses the last option and joins this community. The encounter with other children and the opportunity for communal life brings new hopes for the boy, bringing back his old dreams. Though there is no explicit promise for a brighter future, the world seems at least a little less mournful for the boy who now belongs to a family and a new community.

McCarthy's new world order mingles the conceptions of Turnerian historians and also re-interpreters those of the new western historians. In *The Road*, McCarthy brings up many questions concerning the current and upcoming state of his country—and in broader terms the whole world—which is in a dynamic encounter with former western ideals. He reveals the consequences of a probable apocalyptic devastation in the twenty-first century through a near-documentary description of its survivors in a similar way as Turner described the life and hardships of pioneers building the American nation in the unknown wilderness, or as later Limerick wrote about Native Americans and other ethnicities, and the vulnerability of the environment. McCarthy's novel deconstructs the present world into a horrific imaginary in order to make people conscious about the attendant effects of their politics and of their acts against the environment and one another.

WORKS CITED

Allen, Michael. (Sept. 1994) "The "New" Western History Stillborn." *The Historian* 57.1.: 201-208.

Limerick, Patricia Nelson. (1987) *The Legacy of Conquest: The Unbroken Past of the American West*. New York: Norton.

McCarthy, Cormac. (2006) *The Road*. New York: Vintage.

MacCurdy, Carol. (2010) "*The Road*: Cormac McCarthy's Unmaking of the American Journey." *CrossSections. Vol. 2: Selected Papers in Literature and Culture from the 9th HUSSE Conference*. Andrew C. Rouse, Gertrud Szamosi, Gabriella Vöő. Pécs, Eds: Pécs: Institute of English Studies Faculty of Humanities, University of Pécs, 347-51.

Milner, Clyde A. II., ed. (1996) "Introduction: Envisioning a Second Century of Western History." *A New Significance: Re-Envisioning the History of the American West*. Oxford: Oxford UP, xi-xiv.

Turner, Frederick Jackson. ([1894] 1947) *The Frontier in American History*. New York: Henry Holt.

KENNETH R. STEVENS

FROM COLONY TO REPUBLIC: THE GROWTH OF REVOLUTIONARY CONSCIOUSNESS ON THE TEXAS FRONTIER

"Poor Mexico, so far from God and so close to the United States." These words, according to the legend, originated from the Mexican president Porfirio Díaz. Whether he actually said them is not clear, but certainly many Mexicans had reason to believe it. Mexico in the nineteenth century was a poor country, and the United States was an aggressive neighbor. Life in Mexico was not easy after winning independence from Spain in 1821. The war for independence had introduced economic and political instability. A succession of presidents failed to complete their terms, governments came and went with startling regularity, and strife developed between Federalist and Centralist political factions. The government's inability to maintain order led to separatist movements and civil disorder. Historian David Pletcher aptly described nineteenth-century Mexico as "the sick man of North America" (31).

There was also the ever-present problem of the United States. The Americans were an expansionistic people. They had begun as thirteen English colonies along the east coast of North America and when they achieved independence in 1783, the peace treaty with Britain advanced the western boundary of the United States to the Mississippi River. The Louisiana Purchase of 1803, in Jefferson's administration, added the vast territory extending from the Mississippi to the Rocky Mountains. In 1818, during James Monroe's presidency, General Andrew Jackson invaded Spanish Florida. The resulting Transcontinental Treaty of 1819 included not only the sale of Florida to the United States, but also a boundary agreement that expanded American territorial claims from the Sabine River between Louisiana and Texas northward to the 42nd parallel and as far west as the Pacific Ocean. Americans thought of the United States as an empire. As Thomas Jefferson wrote to James Monroe in 1801, "however our present interests may restrain us within our own limits, it is impossible not to look forward to distant times, when our rapid multiplication will expand it beyond those limits, and cover the whole Northern if not the Southern continent, with people speaking the same language, governed in similar forms, and by similar laws" (Boyd, 35: 719-720). On another occasion, Jefferson informed James Madison that the development of the United States would result in "an empire for liberty" such as the world had never seen "since the creation" (Looney 1: 169).

Mexico rightly saw the United States as a threat to the security of its northern frontier. About 3,000 U.S. citizens had illegally settled in Texas by 1823. Mexico's answer to this problem was the *empresario* system. In 1824, the Mexican Congress enacted a Colonization Law that allowed Mexican states to admit foreign settlers. The next year Coahuila y Texas authorized land agents—termed *empresarios*—who were authorized to select colonists, assign them tracts of land, and ensure that they followed Mexican law. Under that plan Stephen F. Austin, the first *empresario*, known as "the father of Texas," brought in 300 families from the United States. Additional *empresario* grants were awarded to entrepreneurs from the United States and the population of *norteamericanos* grew rapidly. By 1830 there were more than 7,000 immigrants from the United States in Texas, compared to about 3,000 Mexicans. It did not take Anglo-Texans long to develop grievances against Mexican rule. In December 1826, settlers at Nacogdoches, disgruntled by problems over conflicting land titles and a disputed election for the local *alcalde*, proclaimed the Fredonian Republic. The rebellion was quickly suppressed by Mexican soldiers aided by militia from Austin's colony, but the affair troubled officials in Mexico City, some 1,800 kilometers away.

The Mexican government dispatched General Manuel de Mier y Terán on a special mission to study the situation in Texas. One of Mexico's most able military officers, Mier y Terán was ordered to determine the precise boundary between Mexico and the United States along the Sabine River. More importantly, he was to assess the situation in Texas and recommend measures to maintain Mexican authority there. But Mier y Terán's report gave Mexican authorities no comfort. Texas, he lamented, lay "contiguous to the most avid nation in the world," one that in less than fifty years had become "masters of extensive colonies which formerly belonged to Spain and France, and of even more spacious territories from which have disappeared the former owners, the Indian tribes." Rather than "armies, battles, or invasions" Americans simply made claims to more than they were entitled to, followed by the arrival of "adventurers and *empresarios*," complaints about "existing authority," and "diplomatic maneuvers" and "uprisings" that led to the takeover of territory (Jackson, 178; Morton 99-100). Following Terán's report, the Mexican Congress passed the Law of April 6, 1830, which, in addition to increasing the government's administrative and military presence in Texas, prohibited further immigration from the United States and further introduction of slaves. Terán was named director of colonization for Texas, but he pessimistically informed the government "There is no physical force that can stop the entrance of the *norteamericanos*...." (Weber 171).

The Law of April 6, 1830 did much to unravel the tenuous relationship that existed between Mexico and its American colonists. Trouble developed when Col. John Bradburn, a Kentuckian in Mexican service, established the town and fort of Anahuac where the Trinity River entered Galveston Bay. Texans for several years had enjoyed a legal exemption from customs duties, but Bradburn was now determined to collect them. Vessels leaving any port in Texas had to pay customs at Anahuac. The measure was a burden to commerce because to stay within the law, a ship captain at the Brazos River had to travel a hundred miles to pay duties. In December 1831, gunfire was exchanged when three ships sailed from the Brazos without clearing customs. Bradburn also challenged land titles granted by the local land commissioner, gave protection to runaway slaves from Louisiana, and jailed two obstreperous local leaders, William B. Travis and Patrick Jack. Skirmishes broke out between Texans and Mexican soldiers. In a fight at Velasco, on June 26, 1832, several men on each side were killed. The Anahuac insurgents adopted a set of resolutions couching the conflict as a struggle to maintain their constitutional rights.

Events in Texas unfolded against a backdrop of civil disorder in Mexico. The federal Constitution of 1824 had formed nineteen states with Coahuila y Texas as one state. But in the years after independence, Mexico endured a series of political upheavals which reflected a struggle between the center and the periphery; Centralists favored strong government with power grounded in Mexico City while Federalists favored greater autonomy for the outlying regions. As an ethnic minority in a state on the periphery, Texans favored the Federalist position and the Law of April 6 foreshadowed greater control from the center. When General Antonio Lopez de Santa Anna led a Federalist revolt against the government, some Texans favored him even though many distrusted his true intentions. While representing Texas in the Coahuila y Texas legislature at Saltillo in 1832, Austin learned that many Mexican Federalists believed Santa Anna was in fact a Centralist in disguise.

In October 1832, representatives from several Texas towns met at San Felipe and drafted memorials seeking repeal of the ban on immigration from the United States, relief from the imposition of tariff duties, and the admission of Texas as a state separate from Coahuila. They also established committees of correspondence and a central committee for future action. The next month Austin successfully pressed Mexican officials in Texas to forward the colonists' complaints to the national government, but nothing came of the effort because in January 1833, as many had predicted, Santa Anna overthrew the government, imposed a Centralist regime, and nullified the Constitution of 1824.

On April 1, 1833, another Texan convention gathered at San Felipe. The delegates repeated their requests and drafted a provisional state constitution. They selected Austin to present it to the national government in Mexico City. After a difficult three-month journey by mule from San Felipe to Matamoros, then by sailing vessel to Vera Cruz, and via stagecoach over a rough road to Mexico City, Austin reached the capital in July. He explained his mission to Vice President Valentín Gómez Farías and other government ministers, but Congress adjourned in August when cholera struck the city, and Austin himself was among the sufferers.

Congress returned in September, but though it repealed the Law of April 6, 1830, it did not deal with the request for separating Texas from Coahuila. In his frustration, Austin made a fateful mistake. He wrote to the town council of San Antonio, on October 2, 1833, urging that Texas towns to "unite in a measure to organize a local government independent of Coahuila, even though the general government withholds its consent" (Cantrell 271; Barker 2: 1007-1008). When the government learned of the letter he had written, Austin was arrested and jailed in solitary confinement in a windowless cell at the Inquisition Prison in Mexico City. Gradually officials eased his circumstances, giving him less dismal quarters and allowing him visitors. On Christmas Day 1834, he was let out on bail. In May, 1835, the Mexican Congress passed a general amnesty law, and in July Austin was allowed to leave the country. He sailed from Vera Cruz for New Orleans that month, then traveled by ship to Brazoria, where he received an enthusiastic welcome.

His experience as a prisoner changed Austin's views about the place of Texas within the Mexican nation. He had always opposed what he believed were rash calls for independence. After the Anahuac controversy in 1832, some Texans had begun to urge a more aggressive attitude toward Mexican authority. That faction, which included many prominent individuals, became known as the War Party, while Austin and those who favored his more moderate position were termed the Peace Party. The two sides had little use for each other. Even while imprisoned in Mexico Austin had written his brother-in-law James F. Perry that there had been too much of the "ardent, impatient, and inflamatory (sic) impetuosity of passion for the last three years." He linked that trait to the Texan connection with the United States by stating that

> The people of the U.S. are ardent in everything, it is their national character, and what has raised that country to the unparaleled (sic) prosperity it enjoys, and Americans carry the same ardor and enterprise

and love of freedom wherever they go. It is a noble trait of character, but at the same time there are situations and circumstances where *Prudence* dictates moderation and calmness. We are in that situation in Texas. (Barker 3: 17-22).

But after his return from Mexico, Austin began to express a different opinion. He wrote his cousin Mary Austin Holley that "[T]he fact is, we must, and ought to become a part of the United States." It was just as evident, he said, that "the best interests of the United States require that Texas should be effectually, and fully *Americanized*." Just as a "gentle breeze" shakes a ripe peach from a tree, the political problems of Mexico would be the breeze and immigration from the United States would ripen the peach. The greater the immigration from the United States, the more the "political importance of Texas" would be clear to "all reflecting men" and especially to President Andrew Jackson and the United States Senate (Barker 3: 101-103).

Long an influential voice for maintaining ties with Mexico, Austin was defecting to the cause of independence as Texans moved ever closer to revolution. At a reception in his honor at Brazoria on September 8, 1835, Austin told an audience that he had hoped on his return from Mexico to find "Texas at peace and in tranquility," but instead he discovered everything was "disorganized" and "in commotion." The breakdown was "the natural and inevitable consequence of the revolution that has spread all over Mexico," a revolution which had the object of changing Mexico's government from the federalism of the 1824 Constitution to a "central or consolidated one." He called for "a general consultation of the people by means of delegates elected for that purpose, with full powers to give such an answer, in the name of Texas, to this question, as they may deem best, and to adopt such measures as the tranquility and salvation of the country may require" (Barker 3: 116-119).

On October 2, 1835, Texans and Mexicans briefly fought at Gonzales when a Mexican officer ordered colonists to return a small cannon they had obtained years before for defense against Indians. Mexican soldiers were met by Texans who had mounted the gun on a carriage and hung a defiant banner that read "COME AND TAKE IT." In a brief skirmish two Mexican soldiers were killed and the cannon remained with the Texans. Later that month at Concepción Mission, two miles south of San Antonio de Béxar, four hundred Mexican soldiers took significant casualties when they clashed with a militia unit of a hundred Texans who were on a scouting mission. On November 3, 1835, the Consultation began in San Felipe. The delegates voted against declaring independence, but they nonetheless created a provisional government, with a General Council made up of delegates from around Texas, and elected Henry Smith, a

Kentuckian who had arrived in Texas in 1827, as governor. The Consultation established a regular army, under the command of Sam Houston, to replace the haphazard volunteer militia whose officers and men spent most of their time disputing strategy and orders among themselves. Finally, on March 2, 1836, a convention at Washington-on-the-Brazos declared Texas' independence from Mexico.

Meanwhile, a Mexican army of 5,000 under the personal command of President Antonio Lopez de Santa Anna had marched from Mexico to suppress the uprising. Santa Anna, everyone knew, had a much-deserved reputation for ruthlessness. The year before he had suppressed a revolt in the state of Zacatecas and gave his soldiers permission to pillage the city for two days. In addition to other atrocities, more than two thousand civilians were killed. In San Antonio a force of about 200 Texans awaited Santa Anna's arrival in the Alamo, a former Franciscan mission. After a thirteen-day siege, Mexican troops overran the defenders on March 6, 1836. A handful of survivors surrendered at the end and Santa Anna ordered them executed. The dead included not only Texans, but men from more than twenty states in the United States as well as Scotland, Ireland, England, and Germany. The most well-known casualties of the battle were Louisiana slave trader Jim Bowie, inventor of the fearsome knife that bears his name, and American folk hero, David Crockett, of Tennessee (Crisp 103-138). Crockett had served several terms in U.S. Congress, but lost re-election in 1835 and famously bade farewell to his constituents with the words: "You all may go to hell and I am going to Texas."

A few weeks later, on March 27, Santa Anna ordered the execution of 350 Texan prisoners of war at Goliad. The decisive battle of the Texas War for Independence took place just outside present-day Houston on April 21. The armies were camped near each other by the San Jacinto River. At two in the afternoon, Houston's army—with shouts of "Remember the Alamo!" and "Remember Goliad!"—emerged from the woods and attacked. Mexican soldiers, including General Santa Anna himself, broke and ran. The Battle of San Jacinto lasted only 18 minutes, but for two more hours Texans hunted down and killed Mexican soldiers. More than 600 Mexican soldiers died and 730 were taken prisoner. Santa Anna, who had changed into the uniform of a Mexican private, was taken prisoner a few hours later and brought before Sam Houston, who had been wounded in the fight. Many wanted to execute Santa Anna in retribution for the Alamo and Goliad, but Houston declined to do so. As Texas president David G. Burnet observed, "Santa Anna *dead* is no more than Tom, Dick, or Harry *dead*, but living he may avail Texas much" (Siegel 40).

Santa Anna agreed to sign two documents: a "public treaty" and a "secret treaty." In the public treaty Santa Anna promised that "All hostilities between the Mexicans and Texian Troops will cease immediately" and Mexican troops would withdraw "to the other side of the Rio Bravo del Norte" (also referred to as the Rio Grande). In the secret treaty Santa Anna agreed that he would "so prepare matters in the Cabinet of Mexico" that a mission from Texas would be "well received, and that by means of negotiations, all differences may be settled" and Texas independence recognized (Stevens 40-43). After being held for a time in Texas, Santa Anna was sent to the United States where he met with President Andrew Jackson and then was returned to Mexico on a U.S. government vessel. As soon as he was back in Mexico, Santa Anna renounced the agreements. But despite Mexican insistence that Texas was still part of Mexico, San Jacinto settled the question of Texas independence. Just as Manuel Mier y Terán had predicted, American settlers in Texas had made "extravagant claims," followed by the arrival of "adventurers and *empresarios*," complaints about "existing authority," and "diplomatic maneuvers" and "uprisings" that led to the appropriation of territory.

The Anglo-Americans of Texas were indeed the heirs of an aggressive and expansionistic heritage. Equally important, though, Santa Anna's overthrow of the federalist Mexican Constitution of 1824 and his ruthless actions had contributed to the growth of a revolutionary consciousness in Texas and had given American colonists the ideology they needed to justify revolution. In the end the Texas Republic was not self-sustaining. After existing as an independent nation for nine years, Texas accepted an invitation to become a state of the United States. As Thomas Jefferson had foreseen, the American "Empire for Liberty" was advancing across the continent.

WORKS CITED

Barker, Eugene C., ed. (1928) *The Austin Papers*. Annual Report of the American Historical Association for the Year 1922. Vol. 2. Washington: Government Printing Office. Including Austin to Thomas F. Leaming, July 23, 1831, 2: 677-681 and Austin to Ayuntamiento of Béxar, October 2, 1833, 2: 1007-1008.

Barker, Eugene C., ed. (1927) *The Austin Papers: October, 1834-January, 1837*. Vol. 3. Austin: University of Texas P. Including Austin to James F. Perry, November 6, 1834, 3: 17-22, Austin to Mary Austin Holley, August 21, 1835, 3: 101-103 and Austin to the People of Texas, September 8, 1835, 3: 116-119.

Boyd, Julian, et al., eds (1950). *The Papers of Thomas Jefferson*, vol. 35, *1 August to 30 November 1801*. Princeton: Princeton UP. Including Jefferson to James Monroe, November 24, 1801, 35: 719-720.

Crisp, James E. (2005) *Sleuthing the Alamo: Davy Crockett's Last Stand and other Mysteries of the Texas Revolution.* New York: Oxford UP.

Jackson, Jack, ed. (2000) *Texas by Terán: The Diary Kept by General Manuel de Mier y Terán on his 1828 Inspection of Texas* (Translated by John Wheat). Austin: U of Texas P.

Looney, J. Jefferson, et al., eds. (2004) *The Papers of Thomas Jefferson, Retirement Series*, vol 1, *4 March to 15 November 1809.* Princeton: Princeton UP. Including Jefferson to James Madison, April 27, 1809, 1: 169.

Morton, Ohland. (1948) *Terán and Texas: A Chapter in Texas-Mexican Relations.* Austin: Texas State Historical Association. inlcuding Mier y Terán to Minister of War, Nov 14, 1829: 99-100.

Pletcher, David M. (1973) *The Diplomacy of Annexation: Texas, Oregon, and the Mexican War.* Columbia: U of Missouri P.

Siegel, Stanley. (1956) *A Political History of the Texas Republic, 1836-1845.* Austin: U of Texas P.

Stevens, Kenneth, et al., eds. (2012) *The Texas Legation Papers, 1836-1845.* Fort Worth: Texas Christian UP.

Weber, David J. (1982) *The Mexican Frontier, 1821-1846: The American Southwest under Mexico.* Albuquerque: U of New Mexico P.

ANDRÁS TARNÓC

THE "TALKING BOOK:" TRANSGRESSING THE CULTURAL BORDERLINE IN THE WORKS OF JAMES ALBERT GRONNIOSAW, JOHN JEA, AND OLAUDAH EQUIANO

As Michel de Certeau asserts reading without uttering the text is a relatively new experience, one that is connected with modernity since earlier the reader "made his voice the body of the other" (176). Henry Louis Gates regards earlier forms of orality often characterized in the idea of the "Talking Book" to be the principal trope of the African American literary tradition (131). According to Gates, talking books represent a process of textual rendition commemorated primarily in slave narratives including the works of James Albert Gronniosaw, John Jea, and Olaudah Equiano. In a wider sense the motive refers to an encounter of the subjugated or colonized subject with the religious and cultural artifacts of the Euro-American or European colonizer. In slave narratives a common scene involves the pagan or non-Christian slave or Indian who witnesses a European (Anglo) reading or praying with a Bible in hand. Left to his or her own resources after imitating the master's actions the non-literate subject finds that the book "does not talk," or in other words the subaltern cannot read the given text.

Such episodes yield themselves to a variety of interpretations invoking the kind of borders Gloria Anzaldúa speaks of and what here we might call a textual divide. Certainly in this case both physical and cultural borderlines are applicable represented by the passively listening slave and the verbal act of the slave holder along with the meeting of oral and written cultures respectively. Furthermore, the nature or identity of the particular borderline is open for discussion as well. The slave forced to occupy the position of the muted, and the dominant (often Anglo slave owner) displaying agency are separated by an obvious external cultural barrier where each participant in the exchange harbors a hidden internal borderline as well. This essay draws mainly on the works of Henry Louis Gates, Dwight Conquergood, Homi Bhabha, Julia Kristeva, and Yael Ben-Zwi as it attempts to explore these issues while illuminating the cultural, racial, psychological, and social dynamics implied by the trope of the "Talking Book."

The trope of the "Talking Book" first surfaces in the Gronniosaw narrative titled *A Narrative of the Most Remarkable Particulars in the Life of James Albert Ukawsaw Gronniosaw, an African Prince as Related by Himself* (1770). Dictated to a literate white woman or "committed to Paper by the elegant Pen of a young LADY," (Gronniosaw 1770) the text retraces the life of the protagonist from his privileged African background to his eventual life in England. The encounter with the religious and cultural artifacts of dominant European, in this case, Dutch culture, takes place on a slave ship *en route* to Barbados. After his gold chains and other bodily adornments are removed and he is "clothed in the Dutch or English manner" Gronniosaw witnesses the captain reading to his crew from the Bible. Fascinated by the ritual, the young slave attempts to solve the mystery of the "Talking Book" in secret. However, when he opens the book, and puts his ears on the pages it does not talk to him. Gronniosaw's inability to decode the book, that is to make the book talk, has a grave impact on his psyche and the feeling of loss comes upon him due to social and cultural rejection. As he notes,

> I was never so surprised in my whole life as when I saw the book talk to my master; for I thought it did, as I observed him to look upon it, and move his lips.--I wished it would do so to me.--As soon as my master had done reading I follow'd him to the place where he put the book, being mightily delighted with it, and when nobody saw me, I open'd it and put my ear down close upon it, in great hope that it wou'd say something to me; but was very sorry and greatly disappointed when I found it would not speak, this thought immediately presented itself to me, that every body and every thing (sic) despis'd me because I was black. *(1770)*

John Jea's narrative *The Life, History and Unparalleled Sufferings of John Jea* (1811) also contains a similar episode. Jea, born in 1773 and taken from Africa to New York, eventually regains his freedom and becomes an itinerant preacher. He and his family were enslaved in North America when he was two and a half year old. Throughout his early years when he was compelled to work as a field hand he was made to believe that his master is his God. In addition to suffering physical depravation, he was kept, as he writes, in "mental darkness." Similarly to Gronniosaw, he wants to solve the mystery behind intimidating natural phenomena and natural disasters destroying the corn crop and the cattle, he recognizes the divine aspects of the sun and the moon. However, being denied of a god: "Our master told us, that when we died, we should be like the beast that perish; not informing us of God, heaven, or eternal punishments" he searches for the Omnipotent in secret and like Gronniosaw his exposure to Christianity results in a psychological crisis. First the sermons of his minister spark pangs of conscience and Jea begins to see himself as a sinner while assuming the burden of the Original Sin by saying: "I was led to see that I was a sinner; all my sins were brought to mind; and the vengeance of God hanging over my head, ready to crush me to pieces" (Jea 1811). His psychological travails are worsened by the brutal conditions under which he labors and the frequent whippings he is forced to endure at the hands of his master and his sons. The psychological crisis is manifested in incipient rejection of religion, upon seeing the hypocrisy of the master's family: "From my observation of the conduct and conversation of my master and his sons, I was led to hate those who professed themselves christians (sic)" (Jea 1811). In response, he was forced to go to "a place of worship" while his rejection of religion intensified.

Although he begins to pray and search for God in secret, the subsequent inability to find the divine helper results in viewing himself as a sinner in addition to a self-initiated relegation to the status of the abject: "O Lord thou hast made me the off-scouring and the refuse in the midst of all the people" (Jea 1811). After confessing his sins "darkness turns into day" and "ointment of grace is poured on his sin-sick soul" (Jea 1811). At the same time, he is compelled to seek the Lord and it is the words of the Bible heard in church that offer consolation in times of hardship. By the age of 15, he appears to be "delivered from a wounded conscience and a broken spirit" (Jea 1811). While as an indication of being saved he displays his familiarity with the Bible and the town elders are willing to emancipate him, his owner adamantly opposes any effort at liberation: "Thus he talked with me endeavoring to convince me that I ought not to leave him, although I had received my full liberty from the magistrates" (Jea, 1811). Jea this time found shelter from bondage in the church as "he ran from him to the house of God" and was baptized in secret. Moreover, fearing the loss of control over him the master responds to the potential emancipation by excluding his slave from any prospective interaction or communication with the Book: "[he] strove to baffle (him), and to prevent (him) from understanding the Scriptures [...]. He then took the bible (sic!) and showed it [...], and said that the book talked with him" (Jea 1811). Ironically, the master resorts to Ecclesiastes to illustrate that "there was a time to every purpose under the sun, to do all manner of work, that slaves were in duty bound to do whatever their masters commanded them, whether it was right or wrong; so that they must be obedient to a hard spiteful master as to a good one" (Jea 1811). Consequently, just like Gronniosaw, Jea attempts to make the book communicate with him: "so that every opportunity when they were out of the way, I took the book, and held it up to my ears, to try whether the book would talk with me or not, but it proved to be all in vain, for I could not hear it speak one word, which caused me to grieve and lament" (Jea 1811).

While the attempt to deprive Jea from the comfort of Scripture is further intensified by the master's sons' insistence on the maintenance of the cultural barrier, he takes them to task for their apparent superstition, by extension lack of an educated perspective:

> My master's sons also endeavored to convince me, by their reading in the behalf of their father; but I could not comprehend their dark sayings, for it surprised me much, how they could take that blessed book into their hands, and to be so superstitious as to want to make me believe that the book did talk with them" (Jea 1811).

Jea, however, is not intimidated into giving up his search for knowledge, and having acknowledged his inability to make the Book talk to him, he resorts to seeking divine assistance. Being baptized and as such admitted into Christianity, he considers himself worthy for the divine covenant. He says: "after God had done so much for me as he had in pardoning my sins and blotting out my iniquities and transgressions, and making me a new creature [...] I began to ask God in faithful and fervent prayer" (Jea 1811). Having been visited by an angel in his dream he acquires an ability to read the Bible about which he writes:

> the angel standing by me, with the large book open, which was the Holy Bible, and said unto me, 'Thou hast desired to read and understand this book, and to speak the language of it both in English and in Dutch; I will therefore teach thee, and now read" (Jea 1811).

After demonstrating his skill to the magistrates, Jea eventually gains his freedom according to a contemporary law equating the ability to read the Bible, thus being saved, with eligibility for emancipation. Unlike other slaves—such as Douglass who is launched on the road toward literacy by the planter's wife—Jea left on his own was compelled to seek the help of the Lord.

Furthermore, Chapter Three of Olaudah Equiano's *The Interesting Narrative of the Life of Olaudah Equiano* (1789) describes a "Talking Book" episode in a similar way. Having survived the Middle Passage, Equiano is sold into slavery in Virginia. Confronted after the shock of the climactic change (when he believed that snow was salt after his first encounter with it) with the artifacts of Anglo society, his frustration is eased by an attempt to understand his new surroundings from an African perspective—while he serves as a house slave. Unfamiliar with even basic household items and home furnishings, at first he believes that the ticking of a wall clock—which he calls a pocket watch hanging from the chimney—informs his master of comings and goings in the house and of his failure to complete his domestic duties. Equiano also comes to feel that he is being watched by the eyes of a portrait that hangs in the drawing room. At the same time, his *Narrative* contains the now familiar description of his encounter with reading and literacy:

> I had often seen my master and Dick employed in reading; and I had a great curiosity to talk to the books, as I thought they did; and so to learn how all things had a beginning: for that purpose I have often taken up a book, and have talked to it, and then put my ears to it, when alone, in hopes it would answer me; and I have been very much concerned when I found it remained silent (Equiano 1789).

During the Middle Passage, he is intimidated by the culture shock. He recalls that "[T]his heightened my wonder; and I was now more persuaded than ever that I was in another world, and that everything about me was magic" (Equiano 1789); later, when serving as a house slave in Falmouth he attempts to unlock the secret of reading. Unlike Gronniosaw or Jea, who expect books to talk to them, Equiano is approaching the book in secret and initiates the communication awaiting a response. It is also noteworthy that he does not refer specifically to the Bible, as in his description he uses the plural. Consequently, Equiano assuming an active stance by addressing the book and expecting an answer, is not at the mercy of the given text. Having experienced the book's silence Equiano does not become despondent, or pray for heavenly help, he simply registers his resignation and apprehension. Although he is "very much concerned," he refuses to regard his inability to communicate with the book as a measure of his own self-worth.

Another example of this kind is John Marrant's *A Narrative of the Lord's Wonderful Dealings with John Marrant, a Black* (1785) which describes a different encounter. As a young boy lost in the woods John is captured by Cherokee Indians and is taken to their village to face the Chief. Threatened with execution for trespassing onto Indian land, his prayers along with a divinely inspired ability to speak Cherokee spare his life. When questioned by his guard about his familiarity with the law that trespassers onto Cherokee land will be put to death, he responds in his captors' language. Moreover, just before being executed by torture, he prays in Cherokee: "I prayed in English a considerable time, and about the middle of my prayer, the Lord impressed a strong desire upon my mind to turn into their language and pray in their tongue" (Marrant 1785). Afterwards, he is presented to the Chief to whom he recites passages from the Bible. The daughter of the Chief (referred to as "the King") wracked by illness and obviously in need of help attempts to read from the same book, but she finds that the biblical text does not speak to her. After demonstrating his healing powers through prayer: "I besought the Lord again [...] and he was intreated," Marrant's life is repeatedly saved and his words suggest a missionary stance: "the King's house turned to God's house." Furthermore, in a curious reversal of the Gronniosaw episode on the slave ship, it is the Cherokee Chief, who removes "golden ornaments, his chain and bracelets, like a child" (Marrant 1785) at the captive's request. Marrant's status at this point improves dramatically and he is soon welcomed into the Cherokee society. This is how he puts it:

> Now the Lord made all my enemies to become my great friends. I remained nine weeks in the king's palace, praising God day and night: I was never out but three days all the time. I had assumed the habit of the country, and was dressed much like the king, and nothing was too good for me. (Marrant 1785).

In this instance, the main difference is that the parties to the cultural encounter are representatives of two silenced groups. The irony of the situation is that the generally objectified Native American is in a dominant position, while the African, although equipped with the liturgical elements of Christianity, is considered subordinate. Yet, it is the Native American's inability to read or decode the text that leads to a failed cultural exchange or encounter. Despite the reverential treatment, as the chief's daughter kisses the book twice, the by-now familiar result is that the book does not 'talk' to her, that is, she is unable to read it. While the "Talking Book" in the hands of white people leads to the cultural deterritorialization of the black slave, in this case the Indian is excluded from the cultural discourse by the black man. As the Gronniosaw narrative indicated, the self-professed abject status of the slave, whose exclusion from the republic of letters was based on the white master's control of the respective text, in Marrant's encounter with the Indians he will control the given text. In both cases the minority participants are confronted with the idea of potential conversion brought on by the presentation of the Bible in assigning the actual reader or interpreter the role of the missionary. It is also noteworthy that the encounter bears resemblance to the experience of John Jea, as just like the latter's divinely inspired ability to read the Bible in English and Dutch, Marrant is "granted" proficiency in Cherokee.

Episodes or motifs similar to that of the "Talking Book" occur at the same time in texts written by Native Americans as well. In the "School Days of an Indian Girl" (1921) Gertrude Bonnin recalls her travel from the Indian reservation to a Quaker residential school by invoking the motif of the talking telegraph pole. She writes: "Often I had stopped, on my way down the road, to hold my ear against the pole, and, hearing its low moaning, I used to wonder what the paleface had done to hurt it (1644)." At the same time, she describes train travel as a ride "inside of the iron horse" (1644). In both cases, a non-white person's inability to understand modern technology is placed in a racial context.

In all the above instances representatives of groups untutored in the ways of reading and writing are confronted with the liturgical practices or cultural (technological) paraphernalia of Anglo society. While Equiano encounters the problem in relation to books or reading in general and Gronniosaw experiences the "Talking Book" episode after a forceful initiation into white culture, Jea has already spent considerable time in slavery when faced with the problem of making sense of books and reading. On one hand, Gronniosaw (viewing the actions of the captain) is a passive participant in the cultural exchange and his failure to engage the text results in a psychological crisis and an eclipse of self-esteem. The line in which he says that "that every body and every thing despis'd me because I was black" (Gronniosaw 1770) connotes self-hatred, while the ability of reading or understanding the Book suggests worthiness for membership in the WASP community. Jea, on the other hand, is already familiar with the tenets of Christianity; in fact he receives heavenly guidance in learning to read. It is noteworthy that the Book's ability to 'talk' is declared by the slave owner thereby expelling Jea from the "republic of letters" (Gates 2000, 299). Jea's conversion process provides a basis for emancipation which his owner attempts to thwart. The master's insistence on the Book's ability to talk exclusively to him deprives Jea of all the Scriptural comfort he received earlier. Regarding him as an intruder in the Christian community the master delineates the Bible as a forbidden territory or, in Nancy Munn's words, a negative space. However, Jea, does not acknowledge defeat and turns to God for help in reading the Bible and the resulting ability of reading Scripture exclusively will serve as a proof of a miracle eventually leading to his emancipation as he literally reads his way to freedom.

The "Talking Book" episodes offer remarkable examples of intergroup passages. It goes without saying that a borderline exists in between the representatives of the two civilizations, the written and the oral. The encounter tends to be unidirectional, as it is mostly the black slave who ascertains his inability to decode the messages of the Bible. At the same time the "Talking Book" reveals the existence of internal borders as well. Gronniosaw pre-determines his place in the symbolic order, while Jea struggling to achieve literacy and thereby personal freedom challenges it. After the given encounter, the slave approaches the book in secret, thus transgressing across the cultural dividing line. However, the book rejects the reader, and this witnessed practice of communication cannot be re-enacted in reality; thus while the cultural borderline is violated, the cross-border passage amounts only to a sojourn, or incursion at best.

The urge to understand the book also implies an effort to acquire literacy, and of seizing the word. Dwight Conquergood establishes a parallel between the "Talking Book" and the 18th century practice of elocution, an oral equivalent of the enclosures "seizing the spoken word" and "rerouting literacy into oral communication." Ironically, while the slave exposed to the "Talking Book" is in a liminal position, so is the master reading the Bible, occupying according to Ngugi wa Thiongo's *orature* concept, a domain between the printed and spoken word, or speech and writing (Conquergood 147). The theory of orature originally developed by the Ugandan linguist Pio Zirimu refers to the aesthetic value of the spoken utterance. The act of reading out loud or reciting can be regarded as a performance and are thus viewed as the central aspect of orature. However, in this case the identity of the performer and that of the audience are not always clear. Certainly, the slave holder, captain, or any representative of the dominant culture (from the examples above) reading from the Bible performs, but orature requires a participatory audience. In the "Talking Book" context the audience is far from being participatory as the slave, the Indian, or non-white is relegated to passive reception at best.

In another sense the "Talking Book" episode can be seen as an example of Homi K. Bhabha's Third Space, or thirding concept, during which the subaltern modifies the spatio-social paradigm he or she is confronted with. As Bhabha argues:

> It is that Third Space, though unrepresentable in itself, which constitutes the discursive conditions of enunciation that ensure that the meaning and symbols of cultures have no primordial unity or fixity; that even the same signs can be appropriated, translated, rehistoricized and read anew. (55)

Or as Edward Soja asserts, "[T]hird space as an in-between space enables marginals to disorder, reconstruct, and reconstitute the dominant definitions of belonging and power relations" (qtd. in Junka, Rovaretti, 2006).

Henry Louis Gates's notions of "signifying" and the signifying texts is applicable in case of the examples discussed above. These textual examples function as signified versions of those preceding them in the chronological order. Although Milner considers the "Talking Book's" function to self-consciously signify cultural difference and the power of print and reading, the very idea reinvigorates orality. While signifyin(g), according to Gates, refers to playing rhetorical games on texts, Roger D. Abrahams' concept of "a work against which subsequent works in some way react" (qtd. in Gates 74) is instrumental. The ways of reacting can include a mere reference, a reinstatement of a crucial motive, or a repetition of the latter. Consequently, a signifying link can be discerned among the texts discussed in this essay. While the trope of the "Talking Book" first appears in the Gronniosaw narrative, it unwittingly established the guidelines of its future use. The book itself is the Bible in case of Marrant and Jea, and the removal of the gold chain plays a definitive role both for Gronniosaw and Marrant.

The "Talking Book" episodes place the subaltern on a continuum of cultural coping ranging from experiencing, via negotiating, to contesting. The Bible in the slave holder's hand certainly functions as a sign of power. Holding the book entails physical control over the text, and the lack of the slave's ability to read reinforces the slave's marginality. After the slaveholder or master puts down the book, that is, relinquishes its control, the heretofore marginalized person or subaltern attempts to appropriate the text. The passive listener, thus attempts to become a reader, or interpreter of the liturgical lines, or by extension white culture. Consequently, the slave attempting to read or interpret the given text or compelling the book to talk is removed from his erstwhile marginality, and occupies a Third Space between the positions of an illiterate representative of an oral culture and that of the Euro-American or Anglo civilization based on writing. Inspired by Foucault, Bhabha considers the fissures or gaps of the power discourses as a site for the development of the subject. The gap in the power discourse appears, when the master puts down the book. After experiencing the power of the book, the slave negotiates his position, namely the attempt to interpret the text leads to a desire for learning. It is no mere coincidence that both Jea and Marrant report on a divine gift of the ability to read English, or in case of the latter, Cherokee. Accordingly, the slave removed from his African spiritual and cultural roots uses Christianity, the religion of his oppressor, to prove his humanity or identity, in other words, as a means to contest the symbolic order.

Depending on the slave's self-perception and as described earlier the "Talking Book" episode results in the production of "the abject" as well. Julia Kristeva views the abject as the jettisoned, radically excluded object (2). Yet from its place of banishment, the abject "does not cease challenging its master" (2). The Gronniosaw episode illustrates this stance perfectly. By asserting that "every body and every thing despis'd me because I was black," he takes on the condition of the abject. Obviously, he does not wholly accept this status and challenges it soon with the attempt to read the book. While in this case the "Talking Book" functions as a cultural barrier excluding the slave from the republic of letters, the essentialist turn singling out skin color as the potential cause of ostracism, establishes his very identity.

Yael Ben-Zwi argues that texts refusing the black cultural interpreter or reader are participants in the construction of foreignness and the maintenance of cultural barriers, or boundaries (3). In this context, the "Talking Book" episodes, especially in the case of Gronniosaw, trigger feelings of traumatic self-alienation that later are remedied with the subject moving from the status of a passive listener to an active seeker of knowledge. Ben-Zwi's concept of alienating knowledge is applicable here well. "Alienating knowledge creates exoticization by distancing those subjected to it from accessible contexts, representing them as irredeemably foreign, external, and excluded from the non-exotic group" (xviii-xix), writes Ben-Zwi. The slave's resulting inability to decode texts, however, amounts to being denied access to the contemporary epistemes of the given period. Ironically, however, the "Talking Book" episodes above indicate that the process is a bi-directional one—as Equiano considering his surroundings magical exoticizes the culture of the master. Accordingly "he expresses constant amazement at his new surroundings," and "is astonished beyond measure," quite "worried about being eaten," or "sacrificed to the Ruler of the Sea," while any object he saw "filled him with wonder" (Equiano 1789).

In conclusion, the "Talking Book" episodes all have one motive in common, namely the cultural projection defined by Richard Merelman as the conscious or unconscious presentation of images by a social group and its allies to another social group or society (3). Certainly, every such performance involves the reader or person praying and the slave or other submissive party listening avidly. The image projected is of superiority making the given text, the Bible and its messages, at first inaccessible to the listener and thereby representing the power in the master's literacy and the corresponding lack of power in the subaltern's illiteracy coupled with enslavement, a condition eventually condemning him/her to silence and to the status of a marginalized subject. The slave narratives discussed above are examples of counterhegemonic cultural projection, since these texts, including the episode of the "Talking Book," originate from the minority position. The fact that Gronniosaw dictated his text to a white woman ("commited to Paper by the elegant Pen of a young LADY") is also his testimony rendered via a representative of the dominant culture that illustrates the fluidity of the borders of cultural projection. Moreover, the subtitle of Jea's narrative provides a proud reminder of the intellectual and textual ownership of his text that was "Compiled and Written by HIMSELF." Yet, as Jea's master's comments show, the insistence on the book's inability to talk to the slave can be read as a hegemonic operation. The slave witnessing the religious or cultural practices of the master and professing a desire to interpret and process the message of the book breaks away from the oral domain and the subaltern status it is linked to. John Jea provides a very good example of this break as by being denied the opportunity to understand the Bible, he turns the tables on his owners by praying and eventually receiving a divine inspiration to read the Scriptures.

All the cases above represent an encounter of different cultures resulting in an attempt at communication or engagement tied to the given text. The texts discussed above were viewed according to the theory of

Conquergood's "Talking Book," Zirmiu and Thiongo's orature concept along with Bhabha's Third Space theories, Ben-Zwi's and Kristeva's cultural exclusion issues. Although the "Talking Book" episodes all seem to end with a sense that the subaltern's act of communication fails, we must be mindful that the given instances are reported in retrospect thereby providing further reinforcement to the claim that seizing the word put the slave on the path leading to the demise of the peculiar institution.

Works Cited

Ben-Zwi, Yael. (2008) "Ethnography and the Production of Foreignness in Indian Captivity Narratives." *The American Indian Quarterly* 32.1 xi–xxxii.

Bhabha, Homi. (1994) *The Location of Culture.* New York: Routledge.

Bonnin, Gertrude S. (1989) "Schooldays of an Indian Girl." *The Norton Anthology of American Literature.* Eds. Nina Baym et al. 3rd ed. New York: Norton, 1643–1653.

Conquergood, Dwight. (2006) "Rethinking Elocution: The Trope of the Talking Book and Other Figures of Speech." Judith Hamera, ed. *Opening Acts: Performance In/As Communication and Cultural Studies.* Thousand Oaks: Sage Publications Inc. 141–162. Web: http://www.sagepub.com/upmdata/6229_Chapter_5_Hamera_Rev_Final_PDF_3.pdf

de Certeau, Michel. (1984) *The Practice of Everyday Life.* Berkeley: U of California P.

Equiano, Olaudah. (1789) "The Interesting Narrative of the Life of Olaudah Equiano, or Gustavus Vassa, the African." *The Norton Anthology of American Literature.* Eds. Nina Baym et al. 3rd ed. New York: Norton, 307–318. Web: https://archive.org/stream/theinterestingna15399gut/15399.txt

Gates, Henry Louis Jr. (1989) *The Signifying Monkey: A Theory of African-American Literary Criticism.* New York: Oxford UP.

---. (2000) "What's Love Got to Do with It? Critical Theory, Integrity, and the Black Idiom."*African-American Literary Theory: A Reader* Ed. Winston Napier. New York: New York UP, 298–312.

Gronniosaw, James Albert. (1770) *A Narrative of the Most Remarkable Particulars in the Life of James Albert Ukawsaw Gronniosaw, an African Prince as Related by Himself.* Web: http://docsouth.unc.edu/neh/gronniosaw/gronnios.html

Jea, John. (1811) *The Life, History, and Unparalleled Sufferings of John Jea, the African Preacher. Compiled and Written by Himself.* Web: http://docsouth.unc.edu/neh/jeajohn/jeajohn.html

Junka, Laura. (2006) "Camping in the Third Space: Agency, Representation, and the Politics of Gaza Beach." *Public Culture* Spring 18 (2): 348–359. Web: http://publicculture.org/articles/view/18/2/camping-in-the-third-space-agency-representation

Kristeva, Julia. (1982) *Powers of Horror.* New York: Columbia UP.

Marrant, John (1815) . *A Narrative of the life of John Marrant, of New York.* Leeds: Stanhope P, 1815. Web: https://books.google.hu/books?id=CTsKAQAAMAAJ&pg=PA28&lpg=PA28&dq=marrant+john&source=bl&ots=8P3TrnEcl6&sig=KaNRITy7ZkUZjnhleqnwnZZWK8M&hl=hu&sa=X&ved=0CFMQ6AEwBzgKahUKEwjal4-Krq3HAhXMbRQKHcRTCyA#v=onepage&q=marrant%20john&f=false

Merelman, Richard. (1995) *Representing Black Culture: Racial Conflict and Cultural Politics in the United States.* New York: Routledge.

Milner, Michael. (2012) *Fever Reading. Affect and Reading Badly in the Early American Public Sphere.* Durham: U of New Hampshire P.

Rovaretti, Dino. "Invisible Disabilities: Identification within the/a/my Body." Web: http://dinorovaretti.com/files/Invisible%20Disabilities.pdf

Thiong'o Ngũgĩ Wa. *Notes Towards a Performance Theory of Orature.* Web: http://www.ohio.edu/people/hartleyg/ref/Ngugi_Orature.html

GÁBOR TILLMAN

THE RISE OF THE NEW ARTISAN BY FALLING: THE CHALLENGES OF EARLY NINETEENTH CENTURY SOCIETY THROUGH THE LIFE OF SAM PATCH THE FAMOUS JUMPER

On 17 October 1829, thousands gathered on both sides of the Niagara Falls to see Sam Patch jump from a height of 130 feet into the roaring chasm, atop a wooden ladder supported by cables. All around him people kept guessing if he was going to jump, if he was going to survive, if the whole performance was a mere hoax. As it turned out, it was no joke, Sam Patch waited a little, then jumped. The Niagara Falls is among the most spectacular and majestic creations of nature. With its massive water flow and its impressive roar, the Falls attracted tourists from all over the world. After the War of 1812 was over, hotelkeepers worked hard on establishing infrastructure, adding staircases and pavements to turn the Falls into an even more appealing destination. Genteel visitors travelled the length of the Erie Canal to encounter the sublime sight of the Falls and to internalize it as much as possible for later conversations. The rapids upriver from the Falls, however, meant a permanent danger for the inexperienced or simply unlucky boatmen. Since the 1810s, almost every year some locals or visitors had fallen victim to the Niagara, and the number of accounts kept growing with the increase of journalists around. People 'dashed to atoms,' with bodies were never recovered, the Niagara Falls certainly was a place of inspiration and threat at the same time (Johnson *Sam Patch* 105). It was little wonder that the hotel owners decided to capitalize on its fame and provide amusement for a broader audience.

In 1827, visitors witnessed the destruction of the schooner *Michigan* as it sailed down the Falls. It was christened *Pirate Michigan* for the occasion and had live animals (two bear cubs, a buffalo, two foxes, a raccoon, a cat, a dog, and four geese) and human shaped dummies–"pirates"–on board ("Schooner"). Next, in 1829 the organizers heightened the level of entertainment and advertised several programs for the 6th of October:

deafening explosions of rocks into the Niagara, a plunge of the schooner *Superior* and Sam Patch jumping into the Falls. Unfortunately, nothing went the way as originally intended. The explosions only sounded like pop-guns" (qtd. in *Sam Patch* 112) when compared to the deafening roar of the Falls, and the much anticipated final plunge of the *Superior* did not happen because it stuck on some rocks. Patch's jump also got rescheduled for the next day, because he arrived too late and was probably too drunk to do the job as originally planned. He jumped on the 7th, but due to unfriendly weather conditions and the disappointments of the previous day only a portion of the originally expected crowd witnessed it (Johnson *Sam Patch* 112-114). He then proposed a second jump for the 17th of October, and promoted it on handbills in Buffalo during his two-week stay. In the advertisement addressed to the "ladies and gentlemen of Western New York and Upper Canada" he apologized for any disappointment he caused and promised to show his "aero-nautical feats:"

> I shall Ladies and Gentlemen, on Saturday next, Oct. 17th, precisely at 3 o'clock p.m. LEAP at the FALLS of NIAGARA, from a height of 120 to 130 feet, (being 40 to 50 feet higher than I leapt before,) into the eddy below. On my way down from Buffalo, on the morning of that day on the Steamboat Niagara, I shall, for the amusement of the Ladies, doff my coat and spring from the mast head into the Niagara River. (*Sam Patch* 117-118)

Patch kept his promise and dived from the mast of the steamboat *Niagara*. He also appeared later at the base of the 125 foot ladder that was raised below the cliff near Goat Island which bore an American flag on top. He was dressed in a white costume and he "joked that he could not jump or he may get wet. He bowed to the crowd, threw a kiss to the ladies, kissed the American flag" (Rosenberg-Naparsteck 8). What happened after that became a memorable moment in the history of the Niagara:

> Then he stepped to the edge and stood still, and the crowd fell silent. Sam jumped outward and dropped into the abyss. A Buffalo reporter who watched from the foot of the ladder saw Sam fall 'like an arrow into the flood below', and pronounced it a 'matchless and tremendous leap.' From his viewpoint below Table Rock, a Canadian reported that the ladder wobbled as Sam leaped and that he made a sickening half-turn in the air and entered the water with one leg cocked and with a terrifying splash. For endless seconds the crowd stared at the point where Sam had disappeared; a third newsman reported that 'a general burst of 'he's dead, he's lost' ran through the crowd. (*Sam Patch* 122)

There had been others who tried to jump into the Falls, but none of them survived. A boat was circling the spot where Patch disappeared in the water but nobody emerged. It took some time when someone noticed Patch, who managed to evade the curious gazes and swam unseen ashore (Rosenberg-Naparsteck 9). A Buffalo journalist remembered Patch's break to the surface as "a painful and unpleasant, yet indescribable sensation [that] was driven from each breast, by the flood of joy which succeeded, on seeing that he was safe" (qtd. in *Sam Patch* 122). The crowd was cheering; Sam Patch had challenged the Niagara for the second time and survived. For this feat, people acknowledged him as a genuine article, and he became famous nationwide as the first real daredevil. Sam Patch's brief yet unquestionably successful career spanned two years from his first jump on the 30th of September 1827 to his last one on the 13th of November 1829. During this period he made a name for himself.

This paper intends to provide an insight into the mechanisms that made the Sam Patch phenomenon possible, which include the process of industrialization and its direct consequences on society, such as territorial migration, and a migration of artisanship with its inevitable class struggle. Sam Patch therefore was not just a "foolish madman" as writers from the Jacksonian elite preferred to refer to him, but also embodied the shared experience of a larger crowd.

Had Sam Patch not started jumping from incredible heights, his name would have been but a mere record in the civil registry. He evolved into a self-made man quite differently from the Franklinian understanding. He did not write witty memoirs, nor did he contribute to households with inventions. Instead of being a distinguished intellectual he was an average textile worker from Rhode Island. As Seba Smith wrote in the *United States Magazine*: [Patch was not] "a great philosopher, in the common acceptation of the term, like Pythagoras, or Plato, or Newton, or Franklin. Nor a great statesman like Pitt, or Peel, or Webster. His greatness did not lie in this line. And yet Sam Patch was truly great–he was a great jumper" (567). Patch was born in 1799 in Massachusetts but after a series of financial failures his family moved to Pawtucket, Rhode Island in 1807 and eight-year-old Patch started working in Samuel Slater's White Mill (Johnson, "Art" 435). Slater, known as the "Father of the American Industrial Revolution", had come to the United States in 1789. He had a crucial importance in the early industrialization of the States by building the first cotton mill at Pawtucket in 1790. His work force quickly rocketed from nine to one hundred and soon numerous other mills followed suit (Boyer et al. 270). Patch spent the larger part of his childhood working at mills run by Slater and by other businessmen. Throughout the years he had gained experience and had become a boss spinner with child workers under his supervision. In the 1820s, he migrated to Paterson, New Jersey, along with thousands of workers and remained stuck into the life of working class people (Davis 179). He dreamed of running his own textile company and started a candlewick business, but it failed in 1826. A "solitary alcoholic, who beat the children who worked under him" (Johnson, "Art" 435), he must have felt resentment towards the prosperous mill-owner entrepreneurs and he definitely projected his contempt on one of the Paterson businessmen called Timothy Crane.

Crane was a newly-rich Patersonian, who turned a considerable amount of his wealth on various improvements in his surroundings: he bought a piece of woodland along the Passaic River and its waterfall, The Great Passaic Falls, in the hope of reshaping it for recreation of the middle class. He christened the improved place Forest Garden where crowds could have long walks, pleasant conversations, ice cream and could engage in various entertainments, such as circuses and fireworks (Johnson, "Art" 434). Crane had also had a bridge constructed, so as to provide easier access to the Forest Garden. He named it Clinton Bridge after DeWitt Clinton a former New York governor. It was assembled alongside the Falls in September 1827. Once it was finished, Crane "announced that he would supervise his men as they pulled the bridge across the chasm and set it into place" (435). On Saturday, September 30, the factories closed down so that the whole town could come and watch the Clinton Bridge placed over the Passaic Falls (435). The embittered Sam Patch made a—probably alcohol fueled—statement that he was going to ruin Crane's bridge opening celebration. The announcement probably did not take Patch's co-workers by surprise, nonetheless Crane had him locked into a basement to keep him away from the event (435). When Saturday afternoon arrived, the people of Paterson assembled by the Passaic Falls for the spectacle of placing Clinton Bridge.

> The bridge reached the cliff and began riding out over the cables, and then things went briefly wrong: one of the log rollers slipped and dropped end over end into the pool at the base of the falls. The bridge lurched dangerously, but Crane's men regained control and set it safely into place. Crane looked up for applause, but the cheering was broken by shouts from the opposite bank. For there was Sam Patch, standing erect on a rock at the edge of the cliff. Patch spoke to the people near him. Then he stepped off. ("Art" 436)

Patch disappeared in the chasm, and the crowd believed him to be dead. However, after a few seconds he surfaced and swam to the shore grabbing the fallen log roller on his way out of the water. People cheered wildly at the sight. As it turned out, someone had let him out during the preparations, and he took a noble revenge by leaping and stole Crane's show completely (436). Patch's reckless destruction of the celebration can be considered an act of defiance. The incident represented a culmination of latent tensions all over the textile towns (436). This anxiety was present on both social and individual levels. For one, the Forest Garden showed the clash between the differing leisure interests of Crane's middle class and the textile workers' families. The piece of land had already been visited and used for recreational purposes by locals long before Crane bought it. Even though Crane advertised improving the landscape, it meant exclusion from a place that had been used for free. Crane charged a one-penny toll for entering the Forest Garden in order to keep the place decent and safe. Furthermore, instead of his old acquaintances he decidedly and openly invited "the poet and the painter," the "man of leisure," "ladies and gentlemen," "good society," who would behave themselves, and he reserved the rights to exclude *persona non grata*. People with a preference for different kinds of entertainment and not fitting Crane's idea thus became dispossessed. The new Forest Garden provoked outrage among them, and the place was to see long years of vandalism and disturbances. Eventually, Crane gave up his dreams of amelioration, went bankrupt and left (437).

Timothy Crane's passionate enthusiasm for his perception of art was in direct contradiction with that of the average townspeople. He had a romantic ideal that art meant conquering nature and wilderness with civilization and pieces of machinery. He was not alone, "factory owners and the burgeoning American bourgeoisie grandly proclaimed that mills, dams, bridges, and canals 'tamed' the waterfalls, transforming water and rock into a new 'landscape of progress'" (Davis 179). Hence, both the Forest Garden and Clinton Bridge stood as monuments of the grand enterprise of industrial progress. An article in the *Paterson Intelligencer* echoed the same views by claiming: "although Nature has done more for this spot of earth, than perhaps any other of its size, to render it beautiful and interesting to the visitor, it is nevertheless susceptible of very great embellishments, from the hand of ART" (Johnson, "Art" 434). Art, however, had a different meaning for the skilled artisan. Artisans were proud of their skills required for their profession, but the advent of technology affected their trade. In the textile industry, within a few decades there was a transition from the early production model designed by Samuel Slater. His mills in Rhode Island had produced a material that had been then sent out to families for completion of weaving it. Also, Slater had hired whole families for different stages of work. The system was upset by the Boston Manufacturing Company founded by wealthy merchants including Francis Cabot Lowell. Lowell's mills in Waltham and Lowell had more efficient equipment, and they also acquired new workforce. His agents attracted young farm girls to work at the mills, who—most of them poverty-stricken—were happy to escape traditional family discipline, even though the factories meant a different set of strict rules (such as obligatory attendance of the church and curfew past 10 p.m.). Although the fast-evolving economy lacked unions to protect their jobs, as a Vermont teenager put it: "I . . . must work where I can get more pay" (Boyer et al. 271-273). Hence, true artisans had to face devaluation of their work, which also meant a devaluation of their art: if they could not keep up with technology or they did not have the necessary capital they were subdued, their jobs were replaced by machines and unskilled workers operating them. Furthermore, male artisans' supremacy was challenged by young women.

Sam Patch's first public jump opened up, albeit involuntarily, new perspectives for the working class. He reinvented the skilled male artisan thus reinventing his art. Jumping, as an expression of art could not be reproduced by some expensive piece of gear. It could withstand the pace of industrialization as being completely unrelated to it. Yet Patch's jumps were hard to imitate by anybody, as they required skill, determination and quite a bit of nerve (which some would associate with insanity). Young, single and desperate, Patch possessed all the essential attributes. Patch's performances resonated with the contemporary audience on several levels. It was the kind of entertainment the masses were looking for, not the kind that Crane and men like him tried to force on them. Also, it must have represented a glimpse of hope of breaking out of the treadmill for other disappointed artisans. Finally, this was an art that workers acknowledged, as they understood what it took to carry it out. Patch's ability to jump can be defined as a "kind of occupational skill" (Johnson, "Art" 441). This risky habit was not exclusive to Patch, but he certainly refined it to perfection. Most of the textile villages—like Patch's childhood town Pawtucket—were usually built around a waterfall, and while not working, the boys challenged each other into dangerous and reckless free time activities. They jumped from the bridges into the water, each developing his own technique. In Pawtucket, Patch dared to do the most extraordinary feat, which was "a running leap from the roof of a four-story mill, across an embankment, and into the pool" (441). There, he must have mastered the technique of diving like an arrow, feet first, knees slightly bent, and with arms straight to the body.

Rosenberg-Naparsteck states in *Rochester History* that after the first jump Patch leaped over the Passaic Falls at least three times. He realized he could make money with his stunt so after each one he passed his hat around, which enabled him to travel more freely. In August 1828, he jumped at Hoboken, New Jersey from a hundred feet, which was significantly more than the Passaic Falls. After that the papers advertised him as "the New Jersey Jumper" (Rosenberg-Naparsteck 4-5). This performance also marked Patch's departure from his immediate surroundings as he entered the world of show business. This meant jumping for the sake of entertainment without further political agenda (Johnson, *Sam Patch* 76-77). Patch gradually learned to entertain the public: before his jumps he bowed theatrically to the left and right. Before his last jump he even wanted to please local speculations by throwing his pet bear from the same height he was going to jump (155). After years and years of exhausting work in textile mills he could stop moving from town to town chasing better job perspectives. His new vocation included more exciting locations: besides waterfalls, he jumped from ships' masts and yardarms, bridges, and factory walls.

Sam Patch cleverly forged his name into a brand, which constituted of several easily identifiable traits: the New Jersey Jumper leaped with the posture that became his trademark. He allegedly had two upbeat mottoes "Some things can be done as well as others." and "There is no mistake in Sam Patch!" that were later incorporated into everyday language. In addition, he was a patriot who was known to have kissed the American flag as part of his preparation ritual. He also showed his local patriotism by returning to Paterson to perform on the Fourth of July 1828 (Rosenberg-Naparsteck 6). He had another sympathetic gesture towards his former colleagues indicating he still remembered his roots: at his subsequent jumps after the famous first one at the Passaic Falls, he consciously appeared in a uniform, which consisted of a "close-fitting shirt and pants of white cotton. It was neat and highly visible, a good outfit for jumping waterfalls. It was also the parade uniform of the Paterson Association of Spinners" (Johnson, "Art" 442). He sometimes added a black scarf around his waist or neck, thus always carried out his performance promoting the average textile worker. Furthermore, Patch's Fourth of July performance served as a cohesive force for the assembled co-workers. The plain population of Paterson was traditionally ignored during the celebrations of the day, so Patch scheduled his jump so that it coincided with the banquet for prominent members of the town, excluding them for a change (Johnson, *Sam Patch* 66). Soon after the Independence Day celebrations, on the 16th of July, twenty-two Paterson manufacturers issued an announcement about reducing the time allowed for workers' lunch, affecting the lives of thousands. The decision was to be effective on Monday the 21st and caused much uproar; talks of plans of a walkout surfaced instantly. Patch naturally sided with the workers and offered another leap for Saturday the 19th as his contribution to the forming protests. On Saturday, at twelve o'clock the factories and mills closed and about six to ten thousand workers, meaning practically the population of the whole town, gathered to see Patch jump (67-69).

Like many tragic heroes, Patch died at the height of his career. Soon after his publicly acclaimed second leap at the Niagara, Patch travelled to Rochester to socialize. He then wanted to prove his talent again on the 6th of November at the Genesee Falls. Even though his jump was scheduled on a Friday, people left their work and gathered as usual to see him. According to eye-witnesses Patch's jump was both a "beautiful" and a "frightful" sight (Johnson, *Sam Patch* 155). We do not know if he was disappointed with the size of the crowd and money or he simply wanted to ride his wave of success, but he announced a final jump for the next week, before returning to Paterson. The handbill said "Higher Yet! Sam' Last Jump." and featured an eagle in the middle and Patch's trademark statements: "There's no mistake in Sam Patch" and "some things can be done as well as others" (Rochester Public Library). The height this time was increased with a 25-foot platform built on the cliff to make it a 125-foot long jump and this time thousands of people accumulated to see him. As fate would have it, the 13th of November was a Friday and this date brought with itself Patch's last jump.

As he stood on the platform, he waved to the crowd and gave a speech, although its content is a matter of debate. The *Union & Advertiser* claimed Patch had compared himself to great generals (Rosenberg-Naparsteck 11), other witnesses reported his speech being either gibberish, or simply ridiculous. Multiple witnesses stated that he appeared visibly drunk to the extent that later local folklore would not agree on the amount he had consumed before jumping (Johnson, *Sam Patch* 158-159). He jumped all the same, but this time something went wrong: instead of his usual posture, he fell sideways and "slammed into the river with an audible smack" (Rosenberg-Naparsteck 14). The journalist of the *United States Magazine* reported that unlike his preceding jumps "in the last jump he lost his balance, struck the water sideways, and was probably killed by the concussion against the surface" (568). It took some minutes for the audience to realize that something was wrong, then rumors spread that Patch was dead. That day and night boats circled the spot where Patch entered the water but they failed to recover his body. Some blamed the wind, others the alcohol. The reporter for the *Antimasonic Inquirer* printed an article scolding the audience for encouraging Patch to harm his life ("Sam Patch's last leap").

As often the case of suddenly passing celebrities, the public was not yet ready to let go of Patch. Numerous theories about his faked disappearance and sightings of him were circulated. Newspapers posted announcements about him, and some rumors survived even after his "well-preserved body finally popped out of the soft spring ice months later" near Rochester (Davis 177). Moreover, Patch's personality proved to be a dividing line between the supporters of high and mass culture for several reasons. His was a new type of fame; a reputation that was not based on military success, nor was it achieved with nobility in character. He became a celebrity by merely jumping off high objects. Although some journalists almost equaled him to great philosophers, philanthropists and explorers (Smith 567), many Whigs cried out in outrage and considered Patch's success another low-life manifestation of Jacksonian democracy. Journalists often refused to put down his name and rather referred to him as a "crazy chap" or an "insane gentleman" (qtd. in Johnson, *Sam Patch* 92). Colonel William Leete Stone, who reported about Patch's jumps at the Niagara, invented a caricature based on Patch with the name Hiram Doolittle, Jun., which was an obvious reference to the negative character in James F. Cooper's *The Pioneers*. (Johnson, *Sam Patch* 97-98). Patch's life and death proved to be good material for cautionary tales, how not to live your life, and numerous poems spawned joking about his jumps.

Patch left an unquestionable heritage behind his short career, and a different group of people responded to it well. For one, jumping in Pawtucket, Paterson, and Rochester became a local custom until authorities banned it for obvious safety reasons. The name "Sam Patch" found its way into colloquial speech. "What the Sam Patch" and "Where in Sam Patch" could substitute real cursing (Johnson, *Sam Patch* 163). President Andrew Jackson named one of his horses Sam Patch, and proudly posed with him for Ralph E. W. Earl's portrait. A comedian, Dan Marble, toured the country with his Yankee depiction of Sam Patch in the play "Sam Patch, the Jumper". The play's climactic ending included Marble jumping from an estimated 40 to 70 feet, which developed a jumping craze among the members of the audience: "clerks jumped counters, farmers jumped fences, boys and old folks vied in 'doing Sam Patch'" (Dorson). Famous writers like Nathaniel Hawthorne among others stood up for Sam Patch. In his article "Rochester", originally written for the *New England Magazine* in 1834, he muses on Patch's unjust negative reputation:

> How stern a moral may be drawn from the story of poor Sam Patch! Why do we call him a madman or a fool, when he has left his memory around the falls of the Genesee, more permanently than if the letters of his name had been hewn into the forehead of the precipice? Was the leaper of cataracts more mad or foolish than other men who throw away life, or misspend it in pursuit of empty fame, and seldom so triumphantly as he?

Today, Sam Patch's name and legend has probably become forgotten save for a few local patriots who preserved the legacy in different ways: a Rochester brewery, offers the "Sam Patch Porter." Also, starting from a Pittsford pier, visitors can participate in the "Sam Patch Cruise" on board the 1800s packet boat replica *Sam Patch*. Passengers travel along some parts of the Erie Canal while the captain highlights points of interest and shares local history ("A Cruise"). Since Sam Patch's jumps at the Niagara, dozens of people have tried to imitate his success thus developing an obsession with the Falls. Some believed that a barrel of some sort to be the perfect tool for the reckless feat. The first person to try and survive was Annie Edson Taylor, a 61-year-old schoolteacher with financial troubles. She went over the falls in 1901, suffered only a minor head injury, but fortune and fame evaded her, having only earned little money by posing for photographs with her barrel. In 1911, Bobby Leach experimented with a steel barrel and survived with broken kneecaps and a broken jaw. In 1920 Englishman Charles Stephens made an attempt in a wooden barrel with an anvil for ballast. He also tied himself to the anvil for security. Once the ravaged barrel was recovered only Charles's right arm was found inside ("Daredevils").

From the mid-nineteenth century onwards, one way or another, Sam Patch's leaps have spawned new forms of daredevilry. A step back from the Niagara Falls and a glimpse on famous American landmarks suggests that eye-catching recklessness is not limited to the Falls. On May 20, 1999, Robbie Knievel, son of stuntman-actor-daredevil Evel Knievel, jumped over the Grand Canyon with his motorbike broadcast live by a special TV program. He set a personal record of 228 feet and broke a leg during the landing ("Robbie Knievel"). For the Grand Canyon, acrobat and high wire artist Nik Wallenda's "weapon" of choice was a wire stretched on both sides. He walked a distance of 1300 feet across the tightrope at 1500 feet above ground in strong winds and without any safety harness. The televised live event hosted a breath-taking 25-minute walk in which he made it safely to the other side. A year earlier, in 2012 Wallenda had also covered the Niagara Falls, becoming the first person not to jump but to walk over it for a change ("Nick Wallenda"). Additional extreme cases include BASE jumping, such as Jeb Corliss's stunt from the Seattle Space Needle ("Top 10"), as well as Felix Baumgartner's 2012 "space jump" from 24 miles above Roswell, New Mexico (Tierney). These modern daredevils have an urge to conquer famous sights and locations with their insane performances. Thus, Sam Patch made a contribution to the American public after all. With his recklessness he invented the American daredevil and implanted it into the nation's collective unconscious, shocking audiences ever since.

WORKS CITED

"A Cruise on the Sam Patch." Corn Hill Navigation, (2012). Web: http://www.samandmary.org/

"Amazing Niagara Falls Facts." (2012) Niagara Falls State Park. Delaware North Companies Parks & Resorts. Web: http://www.niagarafallsstatepark.com/

Andrews, Evan. (2009) "Top 10 Daredevils." Toptenz.net, 21 Web: http://www.toptenz.net/

Boyer, Paul S., et al. (2004). *The Enduring Vision: A History of the American People. Volume 1: To 1877*. 5th ed. Boston: Houghton Mifflin.

Davis, Janet M. (Jun., 2004). "Proletarian Daredevil: Sam Patch, the Famous Jumper by Paul E. Johnson." *Reviews in American History* 32.2 176-83.

"Daredevils Of Niagara Falls." Niagarafallslive, n.p. n.d. Web: http://www.niagarafallslive.com/

Dorson, Richard M. (Dec., 1966). "The Wonderful leaps of Sam Patch." *American Heritage* 18.1 Web: http://www.americanheritage.com/

Hawthorne, Nathaniel. (1999) "Rochester." Eric Eldred Nathaniel Hawthorne (1804-1864) HomePage. Derry, N.H.: Eldritch Press, Web: http://www.eldritchpress.org/

Higher Yet! Sam's Last Jump. Rochester Public Library Local History Division, n.d. Web.

Johnson, Paul. (Dec., 1988) "'Art' and the Language of Progress in Early-Industrial Paterson: Sam Patch at Clinton Bridge." *American Quarterly* 40.4: 433-49.

---. (2004) *Sam Patch, the Famous Jumper*. New York: Hill and Wang.

"Michigan (Schooner), Sent Over Falls, 8 Sep 1827." Maritime History of the Great Lakes. Walter Lewis, n.d. Web.

"Nik Wallenda: King of the High Wire." (2013) Nik Wallenda.Web: http://nikwallenda.com/

Robbie Knievel Grand Canyon Death Jump. (1999) Perf. Robbie Knievel. Film. Web: https://www.youtube.com/watch?v=NQwdh2Ubfqo

Rosenberg-Naparsteck, Ruth. (Summer, 1991): "The Real Simon Pure Sam Patch." *Rochester History* 52.3 1-24. Web: http://www.rochester.lib.ny.us/

"Sam Patch's Last Leap: Fatal Ending of His Showing That Some Things Can Be Done as well as Others." *The New York Times* (Aug 12, 1883.)

"Schooner 'Michigan'." Niagara Falls Info. n.p. n.d. Web. http://www.niagarafallsinfo.com/

Smith, Seba, et al. (1856) "Life and Death of Sam Patch." *United States Magazine* Vol. 3 July to Dec. 1856: 567-70.

Tierney, John. (Oct. 2012) "24 Miles, 4 Minutes and 834 M.P.H., All in One Jump." *New York Times*, 14.

KRISTIN S. VALENCIA

AMBOS NOGALES: A BRIEF HISTORY

The 1,933-mile long territorial demarcation between the United States and Mexico has become a generative site for critical discussions, both literal and figurative, regarding legislation, citizenship, economics, and social systems. In a literal sense, the U.S.-Mexico border lends itself to discussions of immigration, national patriotism, economic partnerships, border crossing, or state and municipal rollout of federal policies. These topics have occupied the broader and more dominant discourses in news media, social networks, and activist work at different points throughout history – during and after the Mexican American War from 1846 to 1848, during the years of the *Bracero* Program and Great Depression, consistently since the inception of Operation Gatekeeper under President Bill Clinton in 1994, and with heightened border security as a result of the 9/11 attacks. The movement of people through the border on a daily basis, both through legal and illegal means, is demonstrative of the permeability of the territorial line and a consistent contestation to the national identity and nation-state the U.S. has imagined for itself.

Borders are often used as a place of division and seen as the margins of society, not centers of knowledge and cultural production. However, more contemporary research and reevaluation of border regions demonstrates the manner in which borders allow two or more thought processes to interact and open up new modes of thinking and understanding, thus leading to heightened senses of knowledge production, critical thought, and cultural competence. In a figurative sense, the border lends itself to discussions of cultural marginalization, biculturalism, binationality, and border identity in relation to culture, gender, race, class, and ethnicity. The lives of people at the horizontal border involve consistent negotiation in order to maintain the transnational social and economic relationships that extend beyond the U.S.-Mexico divide and consistently rupture the concept of United States nationalism. Those transnational relationships and cross-border connections at and beyond the border demonstrate the ability of the border to join, as much as it separates, lives on the line.

Gloria Anzaldúa describes the place where the United States and Mexico meet as, "*una herida abierta* where the Third World grates against the first and bleeds," a scab does not form, as the interaction between the two countries is in consistent motion preventing complete closure of one side to the other (25). The continuous interactions between the U.S. and Mexico along the territorial divide form a border culture unique to this region, the place that we call *la frontera*, and the people who reside here, *fronterizos*, move between the here and there, taking and bringing cultural and social knowledge with them. A misconception regarding la frontera, is the notion that communities emerged after the placement of the political divide. The historical reality for many of the border communities is that they were once one town or city, split after the Treaty of Guadalupe Hidalgo ended the Mexican American War in 1848, and industry and capitalism allowed one side to grow at a higher rate than the other. The historical connection between the cities and people at the U.S.-Mexico divide is crucial to understanding the interconnected nature of life on the line.

In the seventeenth century, various Spanish settlements in North America were the foundations for exploratory expeditions and settlement of the then, Northern Frontier (Fox 2). This gave way to the migration north due to mining, trade, and economic opportunities throughout the eighteenth and nineteenth centuries. The twentieth century brought the construction of U.S. cities and establishment of borders, which were layered over communities with historically rooted kinship ties and firmly established economic networks (Fox 2). In border cities, these historical relationships maintain the north to south connection and fuel the concept of transnationality by extending beyond the territorial line and connecting, rather than separating, human interactions.

After the signing of the Treaty of Guadalupe Hidalgo in 1848 and the Gadsden Purchase of 1853, the U.S.-Mexico border had been carved out through political means and forced Mexicans, Native Americans, and others in the region to adapt to a new political system. Cities along the borderline were either divided in half or new cities were established on either side to maintain cross-boundary connections. In some instances, the U.S. settlements along the border are merely border crossings with few residents and no city infrastructure. There are various cities on the Mexican side with significantly smaller U.S. counterparts. The largest of the Mexican border cities range in population size from 200,000 to 800,000, and in some cases surpass intentions to determine a static population size, as floating migrant populations cause the number to fluctuate on a daily basis.

Prior to the arrival of the railroad, the border region remained fairly isolated from the rest of the U.S. and cities along the border often had to depend on trade relations with their Mexican neighbors in order to survive. Violence in some border cities persisted through Native American retaliations, "bandits, filibusters, smugglers, cattle thieves, chasers of runaway slaves, trigger happy lawmen, and desperados found a haven on the isolated frontier" (Martínez 32-33). Race relations between Mexicans and Anglos along the border caused tensions regarding manners of conducting business and running cities (33). Residents of the border region encouraged peaceful relations through economic partnerships and social interactions as a means for livable conditions. Border residents had grown increasingly close as a result of the isolation and by the late nineteenth century had experienced steady population and economic growth (33). The border's isolation both from the U.S. and Mexican political centers provided the venue for accommodation and reciprocal relationships to form along the international line (33).

The economic opportunities resulting from mining, agriculture, transportation, ranching, and livestock trade spurred development along the border region. The growth in the border cities, though, is mainly due, "in response to local circumstances that are a function of their border location, tourism, and privileged manufacturing industries," (Arreola & Curtis 14). At various historical moments, the population of the border cities remained static as people and products moved through the border into the larger Mexico and U.S. The ability for border residents to interact with international people and products is an inherent quality of a border identity where switching from social cues in Mexico and the U.S. informs their duality.

Relations between the U.S. and Mexico border residents remained fairly peaceful until the Mexican Revolution when battles at the border would spill from the Mexican side onto U.S. soil. The sense of coexistence and peaceful interactions that led to the border region's development, assisted in maintaining binational relations during the Revolution. The economic partnerships between U.S. investors and Mexican businessmen fueled the desire to preserve peaceful relations in border communities when battles would take place. Porfirio Díaz opened the door for foreign investment in Mexico, increasing the profits in trade from mining, ranching, and agriculture industries (Martínez 34). The Good Neighbor Policy implemented by Franklin D. Roosevelt in 1933, intended to pacify relations with the U.S. and Latin American and Caribbean countries, adding to local moves toward reciprocity. On a national level, though, Latin American countries critiqued the policy for its ability to allow the U.S. to take advantage of market opportunities under the guise of "neighborliness." Debates over the Bracero program in the 1940's and Operation Wetback in the 1950's led to tensions over immigration at the national level, locally, though, residents of the border region worked diligently to retain their levels of coexistence (34).

National debates over immigration extend from the 1920's through our present moment. Implementation of the Department of Homeland Security (DHS) and Immigration and Customs Enforcement (ICE) after the 9/11 attacks on the World Trade Center and the Pentagon in 2001 heightened border security and sought to secure the U.S. borders from terrorist attacks. At the local level, heavier Border Patrol (BP) presence and re-enforcement of the actual fence did not hinder movement as individuals continued their legal and illegal migration through the U.S.-Mexico border. The natural migratory patterns of humans often come with a critique of their ability to maintain rooted cultural connections. When speaking to their social integration, Alicia Schmidt Camacho observes: "Mexican migrants have long sustained traditional households while also pursuing education, religion, and political organization – in short, all the markers of civic life – in the United States," (4). Which points to the elasticity of the border to not separate one culture from the other, but allow for a balance between the two, a cultural coexistence that transcends the concept of a single identification.

In order to examine the local impact of these larger federal interactions, I focus on the connection between Ambos Nogales (both Nogales'), the sister cities of Nogales, Arizona and Nogales, Sonora. Arizona's early history led to its slow development when compared to the steady settlement and growth in the states of California, New Mexico, and Texas. Padre Eusebio Kino established missions throughout Pimeria Alta, the area now known as Southern Arizona and Northern Sonora. These missions led to the establishment of small silver mining settlements, which were dismantled by the Tohono O'odham and Pima Indians in 1751. Roughly 23 miles north of present-day Nogales, Arizona, a garrison was established in Tubac in 1752 that fell under Apache attack leading to abandonment of the settlement. In 1775, the Arizona-Sonora region was primarily used as a passageway during the Juan Bautista de Anza expedition in 1775. In 1841, the Elias family land grant laid claim to the region that is now known as Ambos Nogales. The Gadsden Purchase of 1853 split the city in half, creating Nogales, Arizona, and Heroica Nogales, Sonora. By 1856, the Arizona-Sonora frontier remained fairly unsettled due to this violence, with less than 300 Mexicans fleeing north to Tucson to seek refuge from Apache attacks (McWilliams 82-83). The isolation experienced by the majority of the border region, was significantly greater in Arizona, as it remained distant from the waterfront ports in California and the Santa Fe Trail in New Mexico. This distance prompted those in Arizona to depend on purchasing products and dry goods from Sonora, and merchants in Sonora depended on their U.S. customers. The remoteness, lack of border security, and life necessity laid the foundation for the Arizona-Sonora border residents to develop close-knit transboundary relationships. An estimated 2,000 people remained in Arizona after the Gadsden Purchase and the American Civil War took military troops from the Arizona-Sonora border, leaving the area prone to Apache attacks (McWilliams 82-83). The isolation, coupled with the need to defend their small parcels of land, led to a distinct binational community operating within high instances of lawlessness and violence.

The construction of the railroad from Sonora into Arizona in 1877 connected the Mexican and U.S. states with the opportunity for economic gain previously unavailable to the region (Tinker Salas 116). The area once completely isolated from California and the rest of Mexico, became a port of entry along the U.S.-Mexico border and encouraged a greater reach on exchange of goods from Arizona to Sonora. Mexican agents patrolling the border did little to prevent illegal entry into the state of Sonora, and instead looked forward to the purchasing abilities they would have with the vendor movement through the boundary (116). Merchant traffic shifted and became one of contraband making their way from Arizona into Sonora, though illegal, highly profitable, leading the Mexican government to declare the region a *Zona Libre*, that is, a free trade zone. The relationship between Arizona and Sonora became one of outlaw justice with the merchant trains falling victim to the bandits between Hermosillo and Tucson in an effort to obtain denim, printed cotton cloth, sugar, flour, chocolate, coffee, dried fruit, sardines, rice, and ham (119).

The merchandise being stolen from the trains traveling through the Arizona-Sonora border began to alter the culture at this particular stretch of the U.S.-Mexico border. The diet along the 389-miles began to change, as did the style of clothing, at the same time a new binational market based on the brokerage of goods from Arizona into Sonora yielded new employment opportunities (Tinker Salas 125). A Mexican elite grew out of the connection between the U.S. and Mexican states as international brokers who could bridge the agriculture, mining, and money exchange between Arizona and Sonora established their offices near the boundary line. The transnational nature of the development of this region, rests on the ability of the people living and working there to operate within a transboundary economic and social system. Without the transboundariness of life at the Arizona-Sonora line, the region would not have been able to maintain its strong social ties in the face of political, racial, and territorial conflict.

Prior to the construction of the railroad, the area known today as Ambos Nogales (both Nogales) was called *Rancho Los Nogales* (*Nogal* is Spanish for Walnut tree, of which are still prevalent in the area) under a land grant obtained by José Elías. The land transferred hands between Mexican and U.S. landowners, with little desire for it to be dubbed a city or township. The Gadsden Purchase resulted in the international territorial line splitting Rancho Los Nogales in half. The construction of the railroad had initially been drafted to extend from Mexico north into Texas. The limitations presented by the landscape, cost, and the rate of railroad construction from Sante Fe and California prompted re-evaluation of the tracks from Sonora into the U.S. through Arizona. The 1880's were a time of early settlement in "Los Nogales" by railroad workers and merchants seeking to benefit from binational sales. Legal officials in the U.S. and Mexico saw Los Nogales as a temporary settlement, thought to dissipate once railroad construction was complete (Tinker Salas 149-162).

Nogales did not disappear and the 2010 U.S. Census accounted for a population size of 20, 837 residents in Nogales, Arizona, a number significantly smaller to that of the estimated 400,000 in Nogales, Sonora. The floating population on the Mexican side has been rumored to reach over a million during times of heavy migration, although many residents of the sister cities often consider 380,000 to be a more accurate population size of the Sonoran border city. Regardless of the population density, Ambos Nogales has grown out of a symbiotic relationship as a result of both the implementation of the U.S.-Mexico border and the railroad. The railroad established and linked merchants at the line that had not existed prior to the construction of the railway. The broader discourse regarding border culture is funneled at the Ambos Nogales border site, where specific elements of transboundary social, economic, and political exchanges laid the foundation for binational and bicultural exchanges.

Nogales' primary residents "included a sizeable number of aspiring merchants as well as former government officials seeking to take advantage of expanded ties with the U.S." (Tinker Salas 153). Many affluent residents from Sonora traveled to Nogales during the summer in order to avoid the heat in Hermosillo and Guaymas. Their presence in Nogales incited a desire to establish the border retreat as a city. Early efforts to name the border cities concentrated on their proximity to the border, thus Line City became a popular name, until Ambos city officials decided to retain the original name of the area in an effort to, "underscore the growing interrelationship between the two towns" (Tinker Salas 155). The transboundary relationship that established quickly between Ambos Nogales is evident in Tinker Salas' re-articulation of Brickwood's Saloon, which straddled the border in the 1880's:

> Patrons could evade the laws of either country by simply moving from one side of the room to the other. By sitting astride the border, Brickwood's Saloon, known as the 'Exchange,' developed an ingenious method of circumventing the laws of both countries. For instance, if American customers wished to purchase imported cigars prohibited in the United States, they simply moved over to the Mexican side of the counter to make their purchases (Tinker Salas 156).

For some, the intention was to circumvent the law, however Brickwood's is demonstrative of the ease with which residents could navigate legalities in the U.S. and Mexico. The ideology of the nation-state, when placed in a room in Ambos Nogales, was as simple to negotiate as walking from one side of a room to another. On a national scale, efforts to define the nation's borders were stringent, but in Ambos Nogales, the border was and is permeable and negotiable. In this manner, preserving a local interdependent relationship was more important than adhering to federal laws that did not fully encompass local interests.

Efforts to maintain a harmonious binational relationship were of utmost importance to the residents of Nogales, as they, "spoke of a growing interrelationship with the Mexican town" (Tinker Salas 156). In order to maintain the binational relationship, periodicals from Nogales described the two towns, "as one, for they are really such, being divided by an imaginary line only" (157). Rhetoric regarding their partnership was apparent through various periodicals calling Ambos Nogales friends, partners, and more commonly, sisters. Further indicative of their relationship, was the common occurrence of binational legal matters to be handled locally between Arizona and Sonoran officials in order to avoid outsider or national implementation that devalued local interests. Transfer of arrests was common between the sheriffs of Ambos Nogales, where a Mexican criminal who had traveled into Nogales, Arizona was often handed over to the sheriff of Nogales, Sonora, and vice versa, without the filing of federal paperwork (160-161). Mexican and U.S. officials perceived this local relationship negatively, in particular when plans to build a binational railroad inspection station reached Mexico City. One half of the structure was to be built on the Arizona side, and the other on the Sonoran side. Mexican authorities refused to approve the plans for the structure, however, merchants of Ambos Nogales agreed that, "placing the station astride the border represented good business practices – questions of sovereignty did not intrude into their thinking" (162). The binational and bicultural relationship in Ambos Nogales was perceived negatively for quite sometime, as it was considered a contestation to the nation-states of Mexico and the U.S. It was not until government officials from each country traveled to the border community, that they realized the benefits of the binational partnership in Ambos Nogales.

Merchants in Tucson did not accept Mexican currency as a form of payment, thus relegating Mexican purchasing power to the Nogales port. In addition to accepting funds from either country, businesses, periodicals, and city officials recognized the importance of being bilingual as it would, "double [the] advantage of business and pleasure" (Tinker Salas 158). Many city officials went so far as to send their children to private schools and universities in Mexico City in order to ensure the bilingual capability of the future city officials. As businesses solidified their relationships, social interactions in the form of Women's Clubs, a binational Masonic Lodge, and social clubs were established to bring Ambos Nogales residents with similar interests together (158). The transnational relationship between Ambos Nogales is reflected in an 1893 letter from the leaders of the Masonic Lodge in Nogales, Arizona to the Nogales, Sonora city council president, Manuel Mascareñas, in which they "recognized that petty international questions are almost unavoidably owing to our peculiar international situation. We believe that such questions, not affecting the dignity of either nation, can best be settled among ourselves without involving our respective governments in vexatious international controversies" (158). This form of localized cooperation promoted a strong sense of coexistence and interdependence where residents of Ambos Nogales recognized their binational relationship was difficult for outsiders to comprehend.

The local friendship and camaraderie in Ambos Nogales was most evident during their public celebrations, initially at Christmas dances and posadas, where Arizona residents would travel into Nogales, Sonora to engage in the community events. In 1895, Ambos Nogales city officials partnered to plan a Latin American Carnival, similar to that of Mardi Gras in New Orleans, with elaborate costumes and flour tossing (Tinker Salas 160). This event drew large crowds from Arizona, New Mexico, and Sonora, and garnered attention from the *New York Times*, in which journalists described the event as commendable (160). The success of the binational events prompted annual celebrations in an effort to increase political interaction and generate income from tourism. The public commemorations in Ambos Nogales set the tone for political meetings with presidents and governors from Mexico and the U.S. often meeting in the jovial border town to discuss trade and politics.

The most popular of their annual celebrations became the *Cinco de Mayo Fiestas* or *Fiestas de Mayo*. In order to commemorate the Mexican victory against the French Army during the battle at Puebla on May 5, 1862, members of the Nogales, Sonora community would organize a public celebration that became increasingly popular for their neighbors to the north to attend. The Fiestas de Mayo had been occurring in Nogales, Sonora for a number of years before the Nogales, Arizona community joined in. Chamber of Commerce offices from both sides of the border decided to work together to organize and execute the annual celebration, at times requiring a whole year to plan. The fiesta became steadily significant to the Ambos Nogales community as it increased tourism and highlighted the positive aspects of their border city. Each year the events over the course of the three days increased, creating full schedules of bullfights, parades, ball games, dances, boxing matches, mariachi serenades, rodeos, and a Fiesta Queen Competition and coronation.

Annual interest in the fiestas increased both inside and outside of the community, parade floats were sponsored or constructed by companies from all over Arizona and Sonora. The parade was a key component of the fiestas that demonstrated a binational aspect of the celebration. It began in Nogales, Arizona, traveled south, circled a portion of Nogales, Sonora, and returned to the U.S. side. Just as the parade traveled across the territory line, individuals could move back and forth through the borderline, easily and enjoy a binational celebration of Mexican culture.

On May 4, 1945, Ambos Nogales is described as having a "Christmas appearance" equipped with decorative lights, flags, and everyone in wide *sombreros*. The Chamber of Commerce offices took to ordering decorations and storefront facades constructed by a theater company based out of Phoenix. Attendees of the fiestas were encouraged to dress in both Mexican, Western, or Historical costumes, and those who were not outfitted, would be locked in a mock jail ("Queen Coronation Opens Spring Fiesta on Border; At Nine O'clock Tonight"). Usual city and business activities were halted in order to allow for all to participate in the fiestas.

Young women from Arizona and Sonora would compete against each other for the role of *Cinco de Mayo* Queen. Local Chamber of Commerce offices, city officials, and affluent community members supported queen candidates through fundraisers and socials or dances. At times, young women from affluent families in Mexico, were sent to compete for the crown, as either a means of introducing her to society or allowing her family to develop potential business partnerships with brokers in Ambos Nogales ("Scenes from Early-Day Border Fiestas"). The young woman chosen by the community would be crowned on an "international rostrum," where she would enter on the U.S. side of the stage, receive her crown, and exit on the Mexican side of the stage ("Annual Three-Day Fiesta Opens Here Today: Parade and Rodeo Among Events"). Just as the parade contained a binational component, the coronation further solidified the relationship between both sides of the border with a stage set astride the Arizona and Sonora territorial line.

Tourism to Ambos Nogales increased heavily during the 1940's, as travel to Europe was hindered as a result of World War II. Every year attendance to the Fiestas de Mayo increased, and Ambos Nogales showcased their interconnected nature with city officials, Chamber of Commerce offices, and local organizations working together to ensure the fiesta was planned out and welcoming to all. In 1956, the Governor of Arizona issued a proclamation, which he delivered at the fiestas, and focused on the "harmony and goodwill," shared between "our two great nations," in Ambos Nogales ("Governor Issues Cinco de Mayo Proclamation"). As the Fiestas increased in popularity, the Chamber of Commerce offices worked diligently to obtain permission from the federal government for open passage along the border. In 1960, they received the news that the border would be allowed to remain open in order for fiesta attendees to move freely through the border and without documentation for the duration of the five-day event ("Border to be Open for Annual Fiesta").

Almost as soon as Ambos Nogales had been able to negotiate with national policies to roll out a local celebration, complications with the Bracero Program brought up issues of immigration and a growing national concern for border security. Additionally, in 1963, following the assassination of President John F. Kennedy, the border region experienced federally enforced closures ("Ban on Travel to Mexico Still On"). The proximity of his assassination in Dallas, Texas, to the Mexico border, created a growing concern for his assassin's escape to Mexico. National and federal policies begin to limit the Fiestas de Mayo, and they fizzle out in the late 1970's and early 1980's due to lack of attendance and low funding.

During the 1990's, Nogales, Sonora experienced significant growth as a result of the North American Fair Trade Agreement (NAFTA) and U.S.-style capitalism spurring the establishment of *maquiladoras* on the southern side of the border. The implementation of Operation Gatekeeper in 1994 brought a heavy military presence to the border region, as the United States Army was utilized to reconstruct the actual border fence into its contemporary structure. Cinco de Mayo fiestas and celebrations still occurred on the Sonoran side of the border, but slowly the militarization of the U.S.-Mexico border quieted the overt friendship once showcased at the binational fiestas in Ambos Nogales.

Kinship ties and economic partnerships held strong in the face of national and federal policies, leading local officials to reach for the friendship and camaraderie Ambos Nogales once shared. In February of 2011, Ambos Nogales signed their sister city agreement when city officials from Arizona and Sonora realized the formal agreement had never been formalized on paper. Prior to the institutionalization of this agreement, Ambos Nogales had provided one another with firefighting equipment or personnel and environmental and wastewater services as needed. Ambos Nogales, worked under the assumption that the relationship had been institutionalized at a prior historical moment, as their current interactions were based off of their ability to work together. While the transboundary interactions in many border cities have become distinctly violent as a result of increased drug cartel violence, this has not shaken the interconnected nature of the Ambos Nogales community. As of 2011, the binational Cinco de Mayo Fiestas have been reinvigorated and the city councils of each side work together to hold the Fiesta Queen competition and a binational soccer tournament, with qualifying games taking place on alternating sides over the course of a weekend.

Politically and economically Nogales, Arizona and Nogales, Sonora are still linked as pedestrian travel moves across the borderline on a daily basis to purchase goods, travel to jobs, or attend schools. The mayors of each side often address the community as Ambos Nogales, to indicate the continued partnership on larger political and economic levels. The once harmonious life on the border has been disrupted by drug cartel violence and the perceived threat of terrorist attacks. The characteristics of transnationality are still evident between Nogales, Arizona and Nogales, Sonora, as Mexican and U.S. residents continue to interact at the line, moving through the manmade fence taking and bringing cultural and social cues with them. The characteristics of a border identity are indicative of a strong ability to adapt to continuous change. The current conflicts pose but one challenge to a community who consistently transforms the territorial divide into a bridge, where economic partnerships and bicultural interactions continuously inform their existence.

WORKS CITED

"Annual Three-Day Fiesta Opens Here Today: Parade and Rodeo Among Events." *Nogales International.* 3 May 1946.

Anzaldúa, Gloria. (1987) *Borderlands/La Frontera. The New Mestiza.* San Francisco: Aunt Lute Books.

Arreola, Daniel D. and Curtis, James R. (2003) *The Mexican Border Cities: Landscape Anatomy and Place Personality.* Tucson: U of Arizona P.

"Ban on Travel to Mexico Still On." *Tucson Daily Citizen.* 23 November 1963.

"Border to be Open for Annual Fiesta." *Nogales International.* 15 April 1960.

Fox, Claire. (1999) *The Fence and the River: Culture and Politics at the U.S.-Mexico Border.* U of Minnesota P.

"Governor Issues Cinco de Mayo Proclamation." *Nogales International.* 4 May 1956.

Herzog, Lawrence. (1990) *Where North Meets South: Cities, Space, and Politics on the United States-Mexico Border.* U of Texas P.

Martinez, Oscar J. (1994) *Border People: Life and Society in the US-Mexico Borderlands.* Tucson: U of Arizona P.

McWilliams, Carey. (1990) *North from Mexico: The Spanish-speaking People of the United States.* New York: Greenwood Press.

"Queen Coronation Opens Spring Fiesta on Border; At Nine O'clock Tonight." *Nogales International.* 4 May 1945.

"Scenes from Early-Day Border Fiestas." *Nogales International.* 28 April 1976.

Schmidt Camacho, Alicia. (2008) *Migrant Imaginaries: Latino Cultural Politics in the U.S.-Mexico Borderlands.* New York: New York UP.

Tinker Salas, Miguel. (1997) *In the Shadow of the Eagles: Sonora and the Transformation of the Border During the Porfiriato.* U of California P.

TAMÁS VRAUKÓ

BORDER MUSIC: COUNTRY AND WESTERN ON THE U.S.-MEXICAN BORDER

A lot of city people often regard country and western music as absurd. How can such a genre exist, what is more, flourish, in the 21st century?

In the eighties, Ilene Melish contributed an article to *The History of Rock*, giving the following title to her chapter: "Country Life–Bitter-Sweet Music and Dreams for the Loser and the Little Man" (1641). This music, however, no longer belongs to the "loser and the little man" only; while the music and the songs preserve a lot of their original values, the country and western songs continue to identify with the underdog, and remain usually conservative, sticking to their roots, as the music of the white, Southern working-class people. However, in the meantime, their audience has undergone a major transformation—as have these types of music themselves. As Don Cusic writes,

> [T]he "working class" no longer consists of farmers and manual laborers; today's working middle class still includes those who work with their hands, but their hands are probably on a computer keyboard. Men still wear blue collars, but they may be button-down and come with a tie. (1)

As a result of the developments in modern media, what used to be a local or regional musical genre, is now widely known and can get globally popular. Those who do not think of country music at first when asked about their favorite musical styles, might pretty much like it if they hear as a background for a favorite film. Country music has gradually become popular all over the world among certain audiences, while in the meantime its original audience back home in America has elevated itself into middle-class status. Cusic explains the development in the audience with three groups.

> The three groups that country music has trouble appealing to are (1) the young, who prefer rock; (2) the cultural elite, who prefer classical and jazz; and (3) African-Americans, who often feel the music doesn't speak to them. Some African-Americans (sic) feel the music is racist, many in

100

the cultural elite feel the music is vulgar and smells of the riff raff, while young people in general want to be accepted by their peers, who tend to like the high energy of rock or the pop music of the day (1).

Although the Appalachian Mountains (and region) is often identified as the original place of country music, where Irish, Scottish, and English settlers introduced their folk music, the genre spread to the Southwest with the English-speaking settlers who migrated to these regions. The music of so-called Anglo cowboys and ranchers was, naturally, country music; but these cowboys, who were in relation with the Hispanic people in the area did not restrict their exchanges only to business and commerce; cultural exchange between the Anglos and the Hispanic civilizations covered all areas of life, ranging from clothing through cuisine and music. Albeit Cusic argues that some African Americans consider country music as "racist" in fact, there is a considerable number of blacks who are actually country singers (among them is for example, Charley Pride, Carl Ray, Milton Patton, Scott Eversoll, Trini Triggs and many more). Nevertheless, country singers in the Southwest, at the beginning, proved to be susceptible to Hispanic influence, both in terms of musical styles and its topics. This is not to say that the Anglos did not have prejudices against Hispanics—they did. This fact, however, did not prevent Anglo country singers from adapting melodious Spanish tunes into their own music. Some of the singers, for example Marty Robbins, sang his songs about whitewashed haciendas, manly duels, fast horses, and beautiful *señoritas*—the romantic world of the Southwest as imagined by the listeners in other parts of the world. In exchange, Hispanic singers used Anglo business and marketing methods to sell their own records and to become famous this way. The Texas-born Baldemar Garza Huerta, for example, changed his name to Freddy Fender, borrowing the name Fender from the guitar brand he used. He believed that the 'gringos' would find that name easier to accept than they would with his original name and this would lead his way to fame.

During the first decades of the twentieth century, entertainment, country music and later on, radio, were inseparable from the topics of the border areas. As Curtis Ellison writes,

> [I]n the late 1930s, the Carters lived for three years in… Texas, where they made transcriptions for border "radio" stations licensed in Mexico…. These stations were built just over the Mexican border to avoid legal regulation of power limits by American authorities. Their colorful entrepreneurs […] promoted patent medicines and such questionable health cures as goat gland transplants as a treatment for infertility. Seeking radio entertainment that would attract a broad audience of working-class listeners, these radio innovators employed Mexican balladeers, astrologers, numerologists, fortunetellers, and

> hillbilly and western musicians. [...] The impact of border radio programming in an era when radio listening was the country's most novel form of popular entertainment expanded the appeal of commercial country music. (30)

The topics artists sang about were universal, such as love and romance, but also included stringent social issues, like migration, crime, and adventure, but they also sang about the region and its land. The land that was sparsely populated, and still the home of several cultures that intermingled. This land that was often hostile, put people to the test, but it was still a loveable home that became immortalized in various forms, including the country songs and verses of Johnny Cash: "Through all the thorns and thistles, us cowboys had to go/While the Indians watched upon us, out in New Mexico" (*Lambston*, Johnny Cash). Though Cash had homes in different places (from California through New York City and even to Jamaica), it was in rural Tennessee where he was really able to relax and make himself at home. His famous "house on the lake" in Hendersonville, TN, was close to nature, in an unspoiled rural America where Cash, crossing regional and national borders alike, always liked to return.

For many of the folk and country artists it did not matter if the land they sang about was divided by state borders. For them the land is what it always used to be, an unchanged geo-cultural entity with similar topics that disregarded imposed border:

> The Devil lives in El Paso.
> Well, she has long black hair.
> At night she walks in Los Cayos.
> My advice to you, son, is beware
> Your mother, she got sick down in Mexico.
> She died right in my arms.
> La Diabla was in the corner weeping.
> [...] There's a priest just south of Juarez
> of whom la diabla is scared.
> Have him teach you de la brujería.
> Only then, son, are you safe from her stare. (*La Diabla*, Bob Wayne)

El Paso and Juarez are still the same city, no matter which side of the border you are. In these songs the border walls and fences designed to keep illegal immigrants out do not exist. Here, the devil is a woman; she is sometimes the English Devil, but mostly she is called with the more powerful Spanish epithet, *La Diabla*. Here, and in a lot of other songs from Texas, New Mexico and California, code and language switching is just as natural as it is in prose, poetry, drama or everyday speech.

Woodie Guthrie's song titled "Deportee" did a lot to alleviate the racist charges against the genre and showed that country, too can and is addressing social issues. The song tells the story of an airplane crash from 1948 that transported *braceros*, seasonal farmworkers traveling to and from the U.S. as per a bilateral agreement. They were not "deportees" at all but Guthrie was outraged by the fact that the leading newspapers did not bother to publish the names of the *braceros* lost in the event, only those of the air crew and the American security guard. In the same context, Guthrie also was outraged to find out that American farmers and these *braceros* were paid to destroy good crops in order to keep agricultural prices high. The song was made widely popular by Guthrie's friend, Pete Seeger, and it has been performed by a number of artists since. Its verses say:

> Goodbye to my Juan, goodbye, Rosalita,
> Adios mis amigos, Jesus y Maria;
> You won't have your names when you ride the big airplane,
> All they will call you will be "deportees"
> [...] The sky plane caught fire over Los Gatos Canyon,
> A fireball of lightning, and shook all our hills
> Who are all these friends, all scattered like dry leaves?
> The radio says, "They are just deportees." (*Plain Wreck at Los Gatos* also
> known as *Deportee*, Woodie Guthrie)

It is likely that Guthrie was made sensitive to such events by what is described in *The Illustrated Encyclopedia of Country Music* as his "rural upbringing amid a background of natural disasters" (Dellar and Thomson 102).

The New Jersey-born Bruce Springsteen is seen as both rock and country musician. He is immensely popular with young people who, in Cusic's opinion, mostly resist the attraction of country and western. Springsteen also identified with the underdog status, like most country artists; even the style of many of his songs is very close to that of traditional country music. Gene Santoro describes him as a "neo-folkie," a "Woody Guthrie-meets-John Steinbeck" (224). Nearly half a century after Guthrie, Springsteen also condemns the treatment Mexican immigrants receive on the northern side of the border; in the album titled *The Ghost of Tom Joad* (1995) we find several such songs. One of the most paradigmatic ones is *Sinaloa Cowboys*:

> Miguel came from a small town in northen Mexico
> He came north with his brother Louis to California three years ago
> They crossed at the river levee when Louis was just sixteen
> And found work together in the fields of the San Joaquin
> They left their homes and family

Their father said "My sons one thing you will learn
For everything the north gives it exacts a price in return."
They worked side by side in the orchards
From morning till the day was through
Doing the work the hueros wouldn't do.
[…] Miguel carried Louis' body over his shoulder down a swale
To the creekside and there in the tall grass Louis Rosales died
Miguel lifted Louis' body into his truck and then he drove
To where the morning sunlight fell on a eucalyptus grove
There in the dirt he dug up ten thousand dollars all that they'd saved
Kissed his brother's lips and placed him in his grave. (*Sinaloa Cowboys*,
Bruce Springsteen)

The other significant song in terms of border issues from the same album is *Balboa Park* with verses that depict border matters close to the American border city of San Diego:

He lay his blanket underneath the freeway
As the evening sky grew dark
Took a sniff of toncho from his coke can
And headed through Balboa Park
Where the men in their Mercedes
Come nightly to employ
In the cool San Diego evening
The services of the border boys. (*Balboa Park*, Bruce Springsteen)

Not much has changed during the half century since Guthrie's song: one may work itself to death on the fields, never earning enough, while the border is permeated with drugs, death, trafficking and prostitution. Interestingly, *Rolling Stone Magazine*'s special edition on Bruce Springsteen (2013) contains no reference to the songs on this 1995 album and neither to the others especially that of the album titled *Devils and Dust* (2005). Springsteen's sensitive and actual musical ideas on political and social issues are well surveyed in the publication, even his interest in the situation of Irish immigrants, but paradoxically, there is no reference whatsoever to his songs about immigrants arriving from Mexico and Latin America.

In the 19th century, the Southwest was part of the so-called Wild West, so the gunfighters, outlaws, bounty hunters, sheriffs, cowboys, stagecoach drivers of that period became the natural heroes of the first country and western musicians. In the 20th century, the border zone that is the territory of smuggling, drug trafficking, of legal and illegal immigration continues to provide subject matters for the genre. Some of the migrants the songs tell about carried out a migration of opposite direction: coming from the north, they sought shelter behind the Mexican border. A number of country artists have written and performed songs about these characters and the events surrounding them. From the first, golden age of the genre, Ivan Tribe singled out the most important ones. He said that

> [C]hief among them was the Arizona-born Grand Ole Opry star Marty Robbins (1925–1982), who between 1959 and 1964 had several hit songs that were clearly western in theme and arrangement, beginning with "The Hanging Tree," peaking with the Latin-flavored "El Paso," and continuing with "Running Gun," "Big Iron," "Five Brothers," and "The Cowboy in the Continental Suit." (73-74)

From all these "El Paso" became truly successful, earning the second Grammy Award granted for a country song, but there are other songs by Robbins that have a Latin 'flavor,' too, "Big Iron," for instance, clearly takes place in a Latino environment:

> To the town of Agua Fria rode a stranger one fine day
> Hardly spoke to folks around him didn't have too much to say
> No one dared to ask his business no one dared to make a slip
> For the stranger there among them had a big iron on his hip
> Big iron on his hip. (*Big Iron*, Marty Robbins)

This 1959 country ballad tells about a dramatic duel between the handsome Arizona ranger and a *bandido*, hiding in the town. The description of the duel and the behavior of the local people is so acoustically vivid that we almost see it; it is similar to a scene in an old western movie: the preparations are long and increase the tension in the listeners, but the duel itself takes just a split second.

> It was over in a moment and the folks had gathered round
> There before them lay the body of the outlaw on the ground
> Oh he might have went on living but he made one fatal slip
> When he tried to match the ranger with the big iron on his hip
> Big iron on his hip. (*Big Iron*, Marty Robbins)

In 1988, the border continued to play an important role in the life of those who lived near or somehow with it. Steve Earle's heavy metal-bluegrass combination resulted in a power twang song that reached across various borders, even in Asia, to return to the one in North America. Earle describes this in the following manner:

> I done two tours of duty in Vietnam
> And I came home with a brand new plan
> I take the seed from Colombia and Mexico
> I plant it up the holler down Copperhead Road. (*Copperhead Road*, Steve Earle)

More than a hundred years ago, Billy the Kid (Henry McCarthy or William H. Bonney), the famous Old West gunfighter, was heading for the border to find safety in Mexico. Charlie Daniels sang his adventures in his 1976 song in the following:

> In the southern part of Texas, east and west of El Paso
> Where the mighty Franklin Mountains guard the trail to Mexico
> There's a new-made widow crying and a hearse a-rollin' slow
> I guess the devil's passed this way again.
>
> There's a lathered sorrel stallion running through the Joshua trees
> And a young man in the saddle with his coat tails in the breeze.
> He's got a six gun on his right hip and a rifle at his knees
> And he's dealing in a game that he can't win. (*Billy the Kid*, Charlie Daniels)

In the 21st century there are desperadoes of both genders who do the same: they head for the border, though they know very well that they have no real chance of reaching it, so they also play a game that they can't win. This game is illustrated by Bob Wayne's 2014 country ballad describing such a journey:

> We were shootin', we were swervin'
> Up ahead there was a curve and we was goin' way too fast
> We let off the gas, but that choppa broke too slow
> Threw off the side of the road
> Next to a road sign said Juarez - 20 miles. (*20 Miles to Juarez*, Bob Wayne)

Anglo-Americans often looked upon Mexican women or women living in the border areas as romantic beauties who are there to be ultimately conquered by Yankees. Ronald Takaki quotes a poem written during the Mexican War about such a situation, which is inherent in almost all western movies, too. This stereotype lingers in many western and country songs even today.

> The Spanish maid, with eye of fire
> At balmy evening turns her lyre
> And, looking to the Eastern sky,
> Awaits our Yankee chivalry
> Whose purer blood and valiant arms
> Are fit to clasp her budding charms. (Takaki 178)

The "Spanish maid, with eye of fire" and coal-black hair is still there in the folklore of the borderlands. Marty Robbins falls in love with such a lady in Rosa's Cantina, El Paso. He also sings of her in his song about El Paso.

> Blacker than night were the eyes of Felina,
> Wicked and evil while casting a spell.
> My love was deep for this Mexican maiden;
> I was in love but in vain, I could tell.
>
> One night a wild young cowboy came in,
> Wild as the West Texas wind.
> Dashing and daring,
> A drink he was sharing
> With wicked Felina,
> The girl that I loved. (*El Paso*, Marty Robbins)

A duel for the lady follows, and in the end our hero is fatally wounded, but is granted the privilege of dying in the arms of his beloved one:

> From out of nowhere Felina has found me,
> Kissing my cheek as she kneels by my side.
> Cradled by two loving arms that I'll die for,
> One little kiss and Felina, good-bye.

Rosa's Cantina is a touristic attraction in El Paso today.(Tamás Vraukó's image)

The inside of Rosa's Cantina with country music and cowboy relics. (Tamás Vraukó's image)

Robbins chose this subject similar to the romances in New Mexico called *corridos* (a term for romance also used in Spain) by employing "the rapid movement and realism of the traditional ballad" (Espinoza 128). The folkloristic nature of the *corrido* is often emphasized and in *El Paso* this is obvious. As Aurelio M. Espinoza writes, "[T]he one who composed this ballad is not a consummate poet; he is a poor laborer who lives from his wages. I will not tell my name, not for a whole year. I am just a poor shepherd who tends his flock" (130). However, this is not always true; the authors were very often consummate poets or simply ones that fell into unrequited love—on the border.

The hero of another ballad, Gus, is not as lucky as Robbins. His girlfriend leaves him and runs away with a gambler. Gus follows them in the hope that the girl would return to him, but a Cajun lover from New Orleans is now more attractive to her than poor Gus from San Antonio, Texas. This 2001 song features a one-sided love on the American side of the border:

> Pulled a pistol on the desk clerk cause he would not take a bribe and then he shouted

Give me their number and you might walk out alive
The next thing from the clerk's lips was the number forty-four
And he pointed upstairs and he ran on out the door

He found the room and was ready to go inside
He put a boot to the door and it flew open wide
The gambler he reached for his gun but he would not get a shot
Gus had his aim and he let that hammer drop

The gambler lay before him he was sprawled across that chair
But where was his maiden with the coal black hair
He didn't know she stood behind him, she had gone for wine and bread
He hit the floor when her bullet struck his head. (*The Devil Pays in Gold*,
Jason Boland)

Country has many faces from Kentucky bluegrass through Cajun country to outlaw country in Texas and New Mexico. The latter is also inspired by Hispanic music and culture and alongside with other regional branches, continues to uphold "the values of old myths with harsh realism, defiance and humor" (Melish 1641) even in today's music world.

WORKS CITED

Cusic, Don. (2008) *Discovering Country Music.* Praeger Publishers, Westport, CT.

Dellar, Fred and Roy Thomson. (1977) *An Illustrated Encyclopedia of Country Music.* New York: Salamander.

Ellison, Curtis W. (1995) *Country Music Culture: from Hard Times to Heaven.* Jackson: U of Mississippi P.

Espinoza, Aurelio Macedonio. (1990) *The Folklore of Spain in the American Southwest.* Manuel J. Espinoza ed. Norman: U of Oklahoma P.

Melish, Ilene. (1983) "Country Life–Bitter-Sweet Music for the Loser and the Little Man." *The History of Rock.* Vol. 83: 1641-62.

Santoro, Gene. (2004) *Highway 61 Revisited. The Tangled Roots of American Jazz, Blues, Rock, & Country Music.* Oxford: Oxford UP.

Takaki, Ronald. (1993) *A Different Mirror. A History of Multicultural America.* Boston: Little.

Tribe, Ivan. (2006) *Country: A Regional Exploration.* Connecticut: Greenwood Press.

Wenner, Jann S. (2013) *Bruce. Collectors' Edition.* Rolling Stone Magazine.

CPSIA information can be obtained
at www.ICGtesting.com
Printed in the USA
LVHW050507250122
709254LV00017B/2271